Oil, Land, People
The Challenges for Architecture

Yale School of Architecture
180 York Street
New Haven, CT 06511
www.architecture.yale.edu

Distributed by Actar
355 Lexington Avenue, 8th fl.
New York, NY 10017
www.actar.com

Oil, Land, People: The Challenges for Architecture was made possible through an endowment from the Edward P. Bass Distinguished Visiting Fellowship at the Yale School of Architecture. It is the nineteenth in a series of publications of the Edward P. Bass Distinguished Visiting Fellowship published through the dean's office.

Editors: Nina Rappaport and Charis Armstrong
Text Editor: Cathryn Drake
Design: Manuel Miranda Practice, with Kaming Lee and Fred Pirlot
Library of Congress Control Number: 2025933486
ISBN: 978-1-63840-169-8

Printed in Canada.

Oil, Land, People

The Challenges for Architecture

The Edward P. Bass Distinguished Visiting Architecture Fellowship

Marc de La Bruyère
Edward P. Bass Visiting Fellow

Claire Weisz
Visiting Professor

Andrei Harwell
Senior Critic

Nina Rappaport and Charis Armstrong
Editors

Edward P. Bass Distinguished Visiting Architecture Fellowship

In 2003 Edward P. Bass (Yale College '67), who graduated from the Yale School of Architecture in 1972, endowed this fellowship for property developers to lead advanced studios in collaboration with design faculty. An environmentalist, Bass sponsored the Biosphere 2 development in Oracle, Arizona, in 1991. As a developer he is contributing to the ongoing revitalization of downtown Fort Worth, Texas, where his project Sundance Square, combining restoration and new construction, has transformed a moribund urban core into a vibrant regional center. In his work Bass has been guided by the conviction that architecture is a socially engaged art operating at the intersection of grand visions and everyday realities. The Bass Fellowship ensures that the school curriculum recognizes the role of property developers as integral to the design process by inviting them to work with educators and architecture students in the studio and contextualize the practice of architecture within the wider professional discourse.

The following are the former Bass Fellowship studios:

2005

Poetry, Property, and Place
Gerald Hines and Stefan Behnisch

2006

Future Proofing
Stuart Lipton, Richard Rogers, Chris Wise, and Malcolm Smith

2007

The Human City: Kings Cross
Roger Madelin and Demetri Porphyrios

Urban Integration: Bishopsgate Goods Yard
Nick Johnson and FAT Architects

2008

Learning in Las Vegas
Chuck Atwood and David M. Schwarz

2010

Urban Intersections: São Paulo
Katherine Farley and Deborah Berke

2011

Rethinking Chongqing: Mixed Use and Super Dense
Vincent Lo, Paul Katz, James von Klemperer, and Forth Bagley

Dedication

2012

Social Infrastructure: New York
Douglas Durst and Bjarke Ingles

2013

The Marine Etablissement:
New Terrain for Central Amsterdam
Isaäc Kalisvaart, Alexander Garvin,
Kevin D. Gray, and Andrei Harwell

A Sustainable Bodega/Hotel in Rioja
John Spence, Andy Bow,
Patrick Bellew, and Timothy Newton

2015

Paranoazinho: City-Making
Beyond Brasilia
Rafael Birmann and Sunil Bald

Harlem: Mart 125
Jonathan Rose, Sara Caples,
and Everardo Jefferson

2016

Mixed-Use Regeneration
Jonathan Emery, James von
Klemperer, and Forth Bagley

2017

The Diamonds of American Cities
Janet Marie Smith, Alan Plattus,
and Andrei Harwell

2018

. . . And More
Michael Samuelian, Simon
Hartmann, and Andrei Harwell

2019

Next Generation Tourism:
Touching the Ground Lightly
John Spence, Henry Squire,
Patrick Bellew, and Timothy Newton

2020

The Innovative Urban Workplace
Abby Hamlin, Dana Tang,
and Andrei Harwell

2021

Housing Redux
Nnenna Lynch, James von
Klemperer, Hana Kassem,
and Andrei Harwell

Introduction

Nina Rappaport
Charis Armstrong

Oil, Land, People: The Challenges for Architecture presents the projects created by students for the nineteenth Edward P. Bass Distinguished Visiting Architecture Fellowship. Marc de La Bruyère, the Edward P. Bass Distinguished Visiting Architecture Fellow, Claire Weisz ('89), founding principal of WXY Architecture, and Andrei Harwell, faculty member at the Yale School of Architecture, with assistance from critic Farida Abu-Bakare, director of Global Practice at WXY, led the studio at the Yale School of Architecture.

Set in Edmonton, the capital of Alberta, Canada, the studio investigated and proposed history-conscious proposals for housing in a city poised for future economic growth. Focusing their research on historic and contemporary European housing precedents, the students assessed how climate, economic forces, and urban contexts impacted the composition of housing typologies over time in various contexts. These same considerations then focused on the Canadian housing situation, using Toronto as a case study, before shifting to certain "Gateway Sites" in Edmonton.

Partway through the semester the studio traveled to Toronto, Edmonton, and Jasper National Park while solidifying and honing project topics. In each location the students had the opportunity to participate in tours and conversations with leaders in government, history, and housing development. This on-the-ground experience of Canadian culture informed the development of the students' project strategies. The final studio projects presented proposals that utilized innovative housing schemes and applied socially responsible real estate development to form solutions for local ecological, social, and marketing challenges.

This documentation of the studio opens with a reflective essay by Marc de La Bruyère recounting key impressions from his semester teaching and traveling with the Yale students. The studio design brief follows with the project intent and anticipated challenges. Next is an interview on teaching and housing development by Nina Rappaport with visiting professors Marc de La Bruyère and Claire Weisz. The student research on European and Canadian housing design and development that follows formed the basis for investigations of the project sites indicated in the description of the studio's Canadian travel. Working in pairs, the students' formulated proposals varying in scale, scope, and strategy, which are outlined in five project sections. The book concludes with Claire Weisz's reflections on the real estate paradigms addressed in the studio and their impacts—past, present, and future—on the city.

The editors would like to thank the following students from the class of 2023 for their valuable contributions to the production of this book: Maxwell Baum, Bingyu He, Zishi Li, Andrea Sanchez Moctezuma, Noah Sannes, Jahaan Scipio, Bishrelt

Solongo, Brent Wafula, and Jiaxing Yan. We would also like to extend our gratitude to text editor Cathryn Drake and the graphic designers at Manuel Miranda Practice.

Nina Rappaport
Charis Armstrong

Marc de La Bruyère

The excitement of a collaboration between my partners in teaching, Claire Weisz and Andrei Harwell, and the students illuminated the tension of balancing design, philosophical commitments to sustainability, and the reality of economics.

Claire and I have both lived in Edmonton, the northernmost Canadian city of any size, 600 km from the U.S. border. Long before it became a fur-trading post, railway stop, or provincial capital, the settlement was a meeting ground for the Cree, Blackfoot, Sioux, and other First Nations. Since the arrival of European settlers in the 1780s, through a series of boom and busts the Edmonton region has been a global source of furs, grain, cattle, oil, natural gas, and most recently, "blue" hydrogen.

While it is the provincial capital and home to Alberta's flagship university, Edmonton is a blue-collar city where pickup trucks outnumber bicycles, refineries and energy megaprojects are the order of the day, and tradesmen earning six-figure incomes are the economic pillars of the community. Along with Calgary, a similarly sized city 300 km to the south, it has the highest incomes per capita and the lowest unemployment rates in Canada. Both cities are surrounded by flat prairie and unconstrained by geographic limits, sprawling as far as the eye can see and featuring the most affordable home prices and apartment rental rates of any large city in the country.

Edmonton and Calgary are also susceptible to the vagaries of deep booms and busts. Nominal land prices in downtown Edmonton did not match levels of the 1905 boom until 1976, and the bust of 1981, following a precipitous collapse in the price of oil,

Reflections

Garneau Project and the Edmonton skyline,
Maclab Development Group, Edmonton, Canada,
Diamond Schmitt Architects, 2022

Marc de La Bruyère

led to those same per-square-foot prices dropping by as much as 90 percent in twelve months—wiping out most local developers and several banks in the process.

The Edmonton studio at Yale identified several risk factors in residential rental development that pose a risk to the local economy, including those resulting from a global shift away from oil and gas toward renewable energy; the recent challenge posed by an unprecedented level of international and interprovincial immigration; the considerations of building sustainably in an economy where −40 degrees weather is a regular occurrence in winter; and the impact of limited government support for private-sector rental housing development.

From the early 1980s until very recently, Canada and the province of Alberta have done little to encourage the development of rental housing, let alone affordable or sustainable rental housing. It is no surprise then that, even amid significant population growth, Edmonton features an old and inadequate stock of both market-priced and subsidized rental housing.

Between several days in Toronto and Jasper National Park, the students spent four days in Edmonton meeting with architects, builders, developers, city planners, mortgage brokers, elected officials, and environmental consultants and touring several neighborhoods, infill sites slated for redevelopment, recently completed municipal buildings (recreation complex, library, theater, pool, living historical museum), and the 1905 legislative building.

The students were challenged with considering market needs, risks, expectations, and economic constraints while providing design solutions to address current norms of sustainability, equity, and design. Each group studied the history, culture, and background of the region thoroughly to develop solutions compatible with the expectations of the local context. The results were refreshing and thought-provoking views on the city where Claire and I grew up and had thought we knew thoroughly. One project traced the history of the region back way before the first European settlement to the withdrawal of the glaciers. Two issues rose to the surface: the degree to which Edmonton's economic prosperity relies on the fossil-fuel industry and how that industry's boom-and-bust cycle has led to a culture of impermanence and expediency, both in the built environment and in people's attachment to the city.

With an inspiring degree of thoroughness the student teams developed an understanding of and incorporated considerations of debt and equity financing, market risk,

Drone footage still of Gold Bar Ravine

Marc de La Bruyère

Drone still of the Gold Bar neighborhood and Gold Bar Park, with the North Saskatchewan River in the distance

zoning and environmental restrictions, developer risk considerations, and local and government preferences. All the while they considered the constraints of living in an arctic climate and an energy-dependent economy.

The projects outlined in this book reveal a variety of deeply researched, imaginatively conceived, and thoughtfully executed approaches to real-world problems. As a developer I was inspired to think more deeply about my own projects and about how, together with colleagues and the government, we can consider ways to encourage the kind of future development that will make Edmonton a more sustainable, equitable, and permanent city.

Most of North America's urbanism is thought of as new. This is particularly true of northern and western Canada. This Bass Studio sought to understand the mythologies that have promoted this misconception in order to develop innovative proposals that will address the real issues.

Northern cities in Scandinavia and Canada have seen their populations grow, creating a need for more sustainable and affordable building practices and lower operating costs in the context of extreme climates. Alberta is particularly challenged by its dependence on a wildly cyclical extraction economy, threatened by both the climate crisis and the increasing production costs of its primary outputs, oil and gas. These challenges presented the students with lessons about architecture's relationship to the forces of development and economies.

Since the 1880s the province of Alberta has experienced a series of booms and busts subject to its economic dependence on the fur trade, then on agriculture, and since the 1950s, on extracting petroleum-based resources. This cycle started with the development of the traditional oil and gas industry in northern Alberta in 1948. Since the 1980s the oil and gas industry has made Alberta a desirable place to live, and it has one of the highest average incomes for families in Canada. Yet, with the wild gyrations in the resource economy over the last decades and an increasing consciousness of changing global attitudes toward oil and gas brought on by climate change, some of Alberta's leaders are looking to reorient the province's economy toward a more sustainable future, one that considers Indigenous communities and supports continued growth and prosperity.

The focus of the studio project was Alberta's capital, Edmonton. Located in the northern part of the province, it is one of two principal metropolitan areas, along with Calgary in the south. These cities compete for prominence in a competition that is often compared to Houston versus Dallas. While Calgary is more populous, as the business center of the province, Edmonton is distinct in terms of being the northernmost city of any size in North America, as well as having a low cost of living and high-paying public sector and blue-collar jobs. This is due partly to Edmonton being the provincial capital and center of government, home to the province's premier research university, and near the Athabasca oil sands. In recent years Edmonton has experienced a growing technology sector focused primarily on artificial intelligence, gaming, agri-food, and the development of hydrogen.

Edmonton's northern isolation and its ability to supply workforce housing with minimal government subsidy has made it an ideal laboratory for solving emerging societal challenges.

It also makes for an opportunity to explore new models of development in the Anthropocene era where sustainability, resiliency, and cultural acknowledgment might bring together design and finance. Access to market studies, surveys, and other information concerning project sites was provided by Marc de la Bruyère and Maclab Development.

New strategies for building a realizable and sustainable future were explored in the context of an economy where affordability was not subsidized primarily by the public. So the opportunity to determine what could and should be subsidized when changes are asked of the public allowed the studio to address gaps in social equity, environmental impacts, and cultural opportunity through new development. These possibilities were explored through an architectural inquisition that took the role of design into consideration when harnessing public programs and market forces.

Travel Study Structure

The studio's travel itinerary focused on Canadian experiments in social housing and place by comparing the architecture of workforce housing and communities. Students had direct interactions with leading experts in local government, civic life, business, and architecture through tours and talks in Edmonton and Toronto.

In Alberta the studio had the unique opportunity to experience two environs that shape development—the layers of suburban development around a river valley core and mountain destinations that drive tourism. Both characterize development typologies that are changing through waxing and waning pressures on material sourcing, environmental conservation, and changing political awareness of First Nations' land rights.

Focusing on a housing market that currently receives little or no subsidy allowed the studio to explore new opportunities for integrating affordability with other goals and drivers. The students aimed to investigate what sort of development of buildings and social infrastructure would support generational change and overcome the environmental and social costs of continuing the status quo. In the process the studio considered the following questions:

Studio Brief

How can architecture be part of a solution to sustainable northern development?

What is the pattern of shared places and is there a distinct approach to public space that accommodates broader cultural needs and influences?

What is the role of preservation, adaptive reuse, local material resourcing, and labor in the consideration of long- and short-term pressures on costs?

How can northern design projects become models for resiliency and equitable urbanism?

The semester included shared research initiatives that varied in scale from understanding the history of populations in Alberta and the environments they have occupied to today's regional trends and markets. Students worked in pairs to gain an understanding of current standards in building and urban design through the adaptation and redesign of several sites and properties related to the Maclab Development Group. This work allowed each team to create a position on what advancement might mean and find resolution through the creation of a unique final architectural design of a site and program brief. Their diverse positions would support the architecture evolving the "Gateway" development condition that exists between the center of Edmonton and its suburbs through the development of a "Gateway Site." Each team developed a body of historical and cultural knowledge surrounding two such sites within the Gold Bar and Empire Park neighborhoods. The architectural design emerging from their rigorous inquiry supported the financial viability, environmental sustainability, affordability, climate and social resilience, community well-being, and innovation needed to guide a renewable future for northern cities.

Gold Bar Neighborhood

Containing the sprawling Gold Bar Park and Marc de La Bruyère's family homestead property, the Gold Bar neighborhood transformed across the years from low-density farmland to a suburb housing more than 88,000 Edmontonians. The area is home to a large proportion of homeowners and a growing number of renters. Despite the high density of housing, the area has a majority of single- and two-person households. The renters of the area have average incomes in the $100K-plus range. The area has access and adjacency to natural recreation resources, Gold Bar Park, Gold Stick Park, and the North Saskatchewan River, and retail centers within driving distance.

Empire Park Neighborhood

The Empire Park area comprises roughly fifty percent single residents with a high proportion of "renter-typical" groups and has a critical connection to retail and transportation in the greater Edmonton area. The occupational mix of the area is highly diverse, with community, service, education, government, trades, and transport workers, among others, represented relatively evenly.

Course Structure

The students worked in pairs throughout the semester, and the studio was divided into three main phases. They were encouraged to take a critical approach to representation and narration through a video format that supported traditional architectural production. Video representations incorporated drawings, physical and digital modeling, archival and new photography, and interviews to develop project narratives across the semester.

Part 1 focused on research and class lectures concerning current knowledge around the economic and social drivers in northern cities and societies and the role of architects and culture in development. Design research based in Swedish and Canadian housing contexts encompassed case studies and historical research. A subsequent design exercise allowed students to shape a perspective on a typical large-scale housing development where the site was divided and adapted to allow an investigation of the current types and forms of rental housing in Edmonton.

Part 2 focused on reimagining the kinds of development possible with new standards for sustainability and social impact. Upon returning from the trip to Edmonton, the students reevaluated their initial design studies and narrowed their research interests. The focus of the midterm project was to form a complete adaptation of the "Gateway Site" and present the role of architecture in an emergent city and the environmental issues facing Edmonton as a northern city. This initiated the setting of goals and principles for selecting a final site and outlining a program focus reflecting the value case for each student group's work to frame the scope of the final project.

Part 3 concentrated on using property development tools such as the analysis of a pro forma, site acquisition, and financing potential alongside architectural interventions to negotiate perceived trade-offs between environmental opportunity and the cost of change. Reimagining the project sites through the lens of the preceding design research exercises and their pro formas, the students produced iterations on the relationships between program and adjacency to define the future environmental and financial impact of each project. Acknowledging tangible and intangible constraints, they were encouraged to challenge current expectations for sustainable residential living and embrace the potential for architecture to create a setting for positive social impact. The goal remained to design models with an increased potential to address a great scale of change through a renewable approach.

Gold Bar Neighborhood

Charis Armstrong and Noah Sannes
Andrea Sanchez Moctezuma and Jahaan Scipio
Zishi Li and Jiaxing Yan

Drone still of the Gold Bar neighborhood and Gold Bar Park, with the North Saskatchewan River in the distance

Where the Gold Bar Ravine meets 101 Avenue and Gold Stick Park's ball fields, with the Rivervalley Townhomes seen in the foreground and Eastgate Business Park in the background

Stills from drone videography of the de La Bruyère family's Gold Bar property

Drone still of Gold Bar Ravine

Empire Park Neighborhood

Bingyu He and Maxwell Baum
Bishrelt Solongo and Brent Wafula

Drone stills of the Village at Southgate

Pleasantview Townhomes with the Village at Southgate and the Southgate Center in the background

Interview

Nina Rappaport
Marc de La Bruyère
Claire Weisz

Nina Rappaport in conversation with Marc de La Bruyère, Bass Distinguished Visiting Architecture Fellow, and Claire Weisz, principal of WXY Architecture. First published in Yale's *Constructs.*

Nina Rappaport

Marc, I'm curious about how you first got involved with property development and decided to work for your father's business, after having gone to business school, and your shift into real estate.

Marc de La Bruyère

In my twenties I swore that I would never go into the family real estate development business. So I moved as far away as I could to work for the Paris office of McKinsey & Company and soon realized that management consultants rarely do anything real or concrete. And then, sadly, my father died. Somebody had to run the business in Alberta, and I was the only family member with the skill set to do it. I was supposed to go back for a year or two but discovered that I loved the process of development. I find tremendous satisfaction in providing people with clean, safe, and secure homes. Thirty years passed, and I am still at it.

NR

How has the Canadian environment, both geography and climate, influenced your work?

MdLB

The western Canadian setting is somewhat particular. Thanks to the importance of the oil patch on the local economy, Edmonton is one the last bastions of well-paying blue-collar jobs: plumbers, electricians, carpenters, and welders are able to earn a great deal of money compared to their peers in the rest of the world. Because of this Alberta has the highest GDP per capita in Canada and, arguably, in North America. It's also isolated and very cold in winter, so people tend to focus a great deal on the attractiveness and quality of their homes. While there isn't high aesthetic experimentation, there's a very strong focus on quality construction. Lastly, the real estate development community is very local, so you are always working with the same people, and reputation really matters.

NR

Claire, having also grown up in Edmonton, how has the Canadian environment influenced your work and the trajectory of your firm in New York?

Claire Weisz

I am one of those people—of which there are many millions—who leave the place where they grew up to make a life somewhere else. So I only really know Edmonton as I left it, after high school. My family is still there, and I visit them often. But I haven't gone there in my capacity as an architect, so this Yale studio will give me a perspective as well. In many ways it's no different than growing up in a place like Texas, which has an economy based on extraction with boom-and-bust cycles. My migration to the United States is a result of one of those bust cycles.

NR

In terms of your practice, you've been very focused on public projects in New York City as both architects and urban designers. What is your model for the practice, and what inspired you to go in that direction?

CW

I would say that my interest in public space was a reaction to watching the creation of the West Edmonton Mall through the destruction of downtown. My professional degree is from the University of Toronto, with my thesis project focused on Edmonton. The thesis was that it should be possible to design microclimate-forward districts with streets and markets designed for people to enjoy in the winter. We had access to RWDI, an engineering company, where you could shape spaces to see how to reduce the snow buildup and alleviate the effects of wind. I focused on climate as well as how to use the city to shape better situations, which is not so distant from what I've ended up doing.

NR

Marc, how do you respond to the climate issues in development and architecture in Alberta? Are you finding ways to address some of the tougher environmental and sustainability issues with your projects?

MdLB

Two things Claire mentioned are important to me and to our Yale studio: first is the impact of the boom-and-bust cycle. I graduated from university in 1982, just in time for the bust, when everything in Alberta came to a grinding halt. There is a visible construction gap between 1982 and '92, when the economy began to recover. The second is our planning department: in the past, in part because of the instability, Edmonton

Nina Rappaport
Marc de La Bruyère
Claire Weisz

City Planning has been dysfunctional. Even now the agency does not always think through ideas fully. As a developer you swim in these challenging currents. One of the good things is that the city has invested heavily in a light rail transit (LRT) system in the past ten years. I've been developing traditional suburban neighborhoods, and in response to LRT investment I am focusing on high-rise residential projects at LRT stops, which will free people from car dependency.

NR

Claire, with your focus on the need to be proactive in urban development and public space initiatives, what project have you worked on with a city agency recently that had a successful direction for residents?

CW

I'm extremely interested in public involvement and public-private partnerships, starting from the Design Trust for Public Space—whether firms, developers, landowners, or city officials, people have a lot to contribute. The city had put out a request for proposals to reimagine a live-work campus on the former Spofford Juvenile Detention Center, in Hunts Point, Bronx. Three different developers, one a nonprofit and two for-profit, created a team with WXY, Body Lawson Associates, and Elizabeth Kennedy Landscape Architect. It was a long process with a lot of agencies. What is new is affordable manufacturing with affordable housing. The project includes 800 housing units, and it all had to be rezoned. The first phase opened in July, and there will be three more buildings. At the ribbon cutting they joked that it was the fastest rezoning the city has accomplished. It had a lot to do with the alignment of goals and the right architectural and urban design construct. The site was complicated because it has a rocky outcropping and needed a destiny. As an architect, being able to change destiny is exciting.

NR

Marc, what have been the biggest challenges for you in terms of your work and the way you have engaged with a community in the approval process for your new residential towers?

Robert R. Douglass Bridge, WXY Architecture and Urban Design with Thornton Tomasetti, Manhattan, NY, 2020
Photography by Albert Vecerka/Esto

Nina Rappaport
Marc de La Bruyère
Claire Weisz

Arverne East Welcome Center, WXY Architecture and Urban Design, Queens, NY, 2023
Photography by Albert Vecerka/Esto

DSNY Salt Shed and Garage, WXY Architecture and Urban Design with Dattner Architects, New York, NY, 2016
Photography by Albert Vecerka/Esto

Nina Rappaport
Marc de La Bruyère
Claire Weisz

MdLB

I think development is actually easy if you're willing to listen and work with the community. For instance one of the most important drivers of Edmonton is the University of Alberta. It is a classic land-grant university with more than 40,000 students and 1,000 faculty members. As is often the case, there is a certain level of distrust among the adjacent communities, the university, and developers working in the area. Over many years I assembled a fabulous parcel across the street from the university within a couple of blocks of an LRT station. We spent a great deal of time talking with and listening to members of the community to understand their needs and concerns vis-à-vis development and the university. By the time we asked the city council for approval we had the unanimous support of every community organization in the area. The head of the local community group gave me a big hug when our rezoning was approved, and the mayor stopped the proceedings and said, "Excuse me, this is a crime against nature that the community is on good terms with the developer." It really isn't hard: you spend time and effort listening and sincerely trying to figure out your partner's needs, and then provide them. The challenge is doing your part sensitively.

NR

Do you have a project that changed because of the community's local knowledge and responses to your design, the site, or the composition of the neighborhood? Is there a situation where the community actually had design input?

MdLB

In Garneau we have two towers, one a student residence built on a commercial podium fronting a somewhat bland streetscape. The community wanted three-bedroom family housing and street-level energy. So we built in a row of town houses that make the streetscape much more attractive and will bring in a nice mix of residents. In a current project development, The Parks, the community was in favor of moving away from the traditional one-bedroom and studio model for two and three bedrooms, which will make a stronger community.

Nina Rappaport
Marc de La Bruyère
Claire Weisz

NR

In a similar vein, Claire, have you changed the brief for a project that either the city or a developer has handed you or engaged with a community issue that wasn't evident before, perhaps responding to a project with an alternative process?

CW

In most cases what we want to do is help create or change a relationship between a public agency and a community based on the possibility for a new design. By the time architects show up they get told what the problem is, for example: "I want this space to be taller." But no one asks, "Why do you need the space to be taller? Is it because of previous experiences or a need?" So discovering the problem behind the request is part of engagement. For our SeaGlass Carousel, in The Battery, we discovered that women, in particular, were scared to go into the park. So the question was, "How do we attract people to go there?" Often you begin a project by figuring out the problem behind the problem. It turns out that when people see activity or lights inside spaces, they get intrigued. Then they might also go there for other reasons. If it were easy to make change with design, then it would be happening all the time, but the truth is that change is extremely slow.

NR

Marc, why does design matter to you, and what part of the design process is most important in your development projects?

MdLB

Design always matters. One of the peculiarities of our firm is that we build and hold; we still own residential rental projects that were developed in the 1950s. I know third-generation families living in our properties. When you know that something is going to be part of the rest of your life, and perhaps those of your children, you have an incentive to design it to remain livable through several cycles of fashion. It's worth every effort and every bit of money to invest in design up front.

NR

What new projects are you each working on now?

Garneau Project, Maclab Development Group with Diamond Schmitt Architects, Edmonton, Canada, 2022

Nina Rappaport
Marc de La Bruyère
Claire Weisz

MdLB

One site is the 1905 farm homestead where I grew up. My family and I have moved out, and I'm trying to develop and preserve the property. Another is a 25-acre site of 60-year-old low-density multifamily residential rental units that should be higher density and mixed-use, and the third is to transform a dying shopping mall on the LRT Line.

CW

We are working on a big range of projects in places that need a fresh approach, from reimagining the river-front in downtown Toledo, Ohio, to updating the BAM Rose Cinemas. Then there are projects that add new buildings and programs to challenging sites, such as an Environmental Hub in Far Rockaway, a passive affordable-housing development in East Harlem, and a school building for community offices from our 2019 Harlem Community Plan. We are also working on the Storm King Art Center with hparc (Heneghan Peng Architects) and a resiliency project for the Robert Rauschenberg Foundation.

NR

What is the focus of your studio at Yale in terms of building typology and context?

CW

We have titled the studio "Oil, Land, People: The Challenges for Architecture." It is a Canadian-focused studio, but we hope it's going to provide lessons for architecture in what development and the built environment can do in terms of changing our economy relative to oil and gas. It will be important to examine building types in Toronto, Edmonton, and Jasper, in the mountains—the other reason people move to Alberta.

Experiments in Housing: Case Studies in Sweden and Canada

Experiments in Housing: Case Studies in Sweden

The first assignment of the studio's housing-research phase asked pairs of students to analyze the evolution of successful community models focused on economic stability at the urban scale in Sweden. Choosing from five urban examples, two 1960s projects and three contemporary projects, the students studied and discussed the architectural language of place and how progressive and reactionary design choices reflect culture. A series of mappings, planning/design analyses, and imagery revealed architecture as a conveyor of content and context in civic life. These works built toward the next step in the students' understanding of the Canadian context and what might differentiate it from other northern cities.

Årsta District Stockholm 1935–45

Noah Sannes
and Charis Armstrong

In the 1930s Sweden faced an economic depression that triggered a period of historically low birth rates due in large part to the lack of affordable housing and childcare.[1] Influenced by public-housing movements in Germany, the Barnrikehus ("child-rich house") in Årsta promoted larger families through requiring applicants to have at least three children to qualify.[2] The housing was considered widely successful because its design promoted a supportive community and seasonal comfort.[3]

1 Ekonomifakta, "From War to the Swedish Model," ekonomifakta.se/en/swedish-economic-history.

2 Stockholmskallan, stockholmskallan.stockholm.se/post/33569.

3 Ekonomifakta, "From War."

Årsta location in relation to Stockholm

Årsta neighborhood map and entry points to buildings

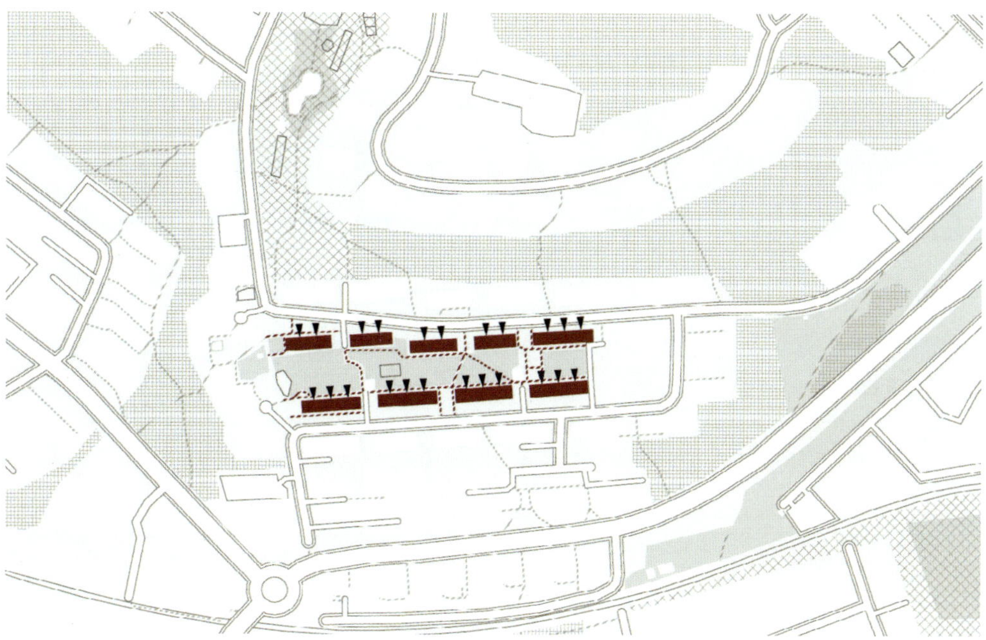

Årsta District Stockholm 1935–45

Noah Sannes and Charis Armstrong

Elevation studies

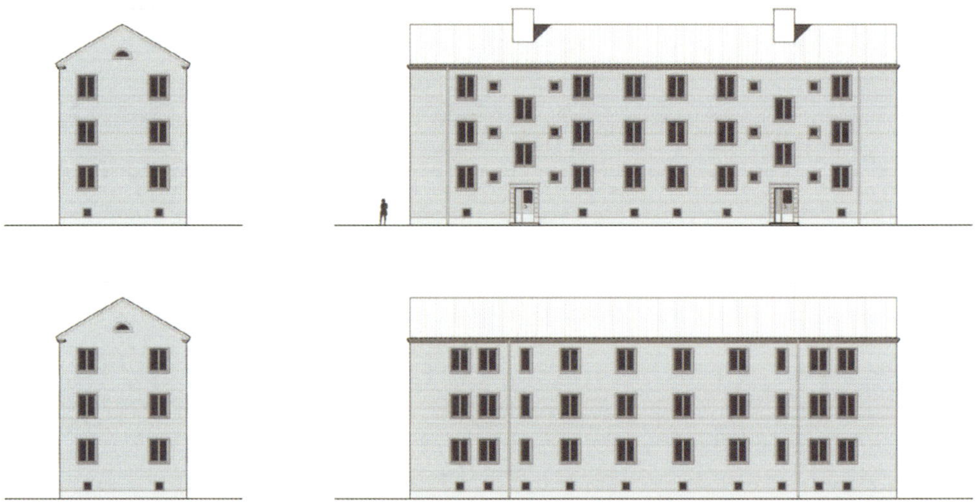

Årsta Barnrikehus typical plan

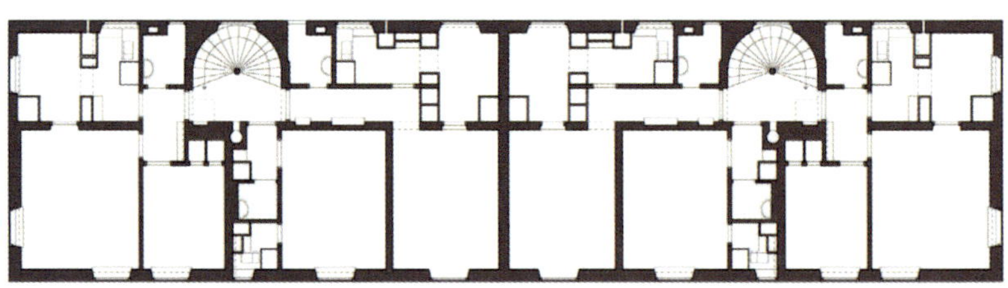

Ventilation scheme

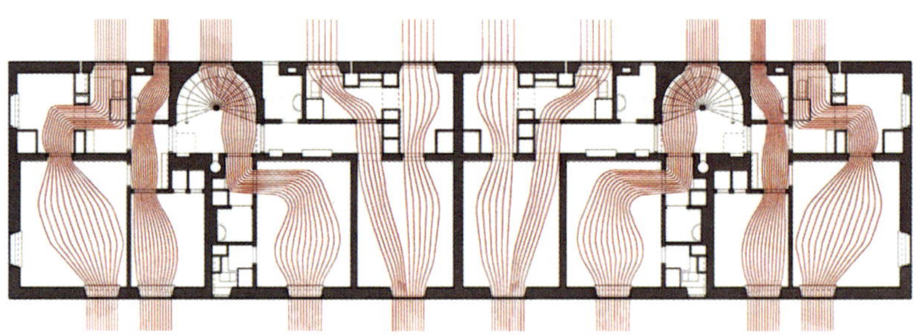

Sun-shading and ventilation scheme

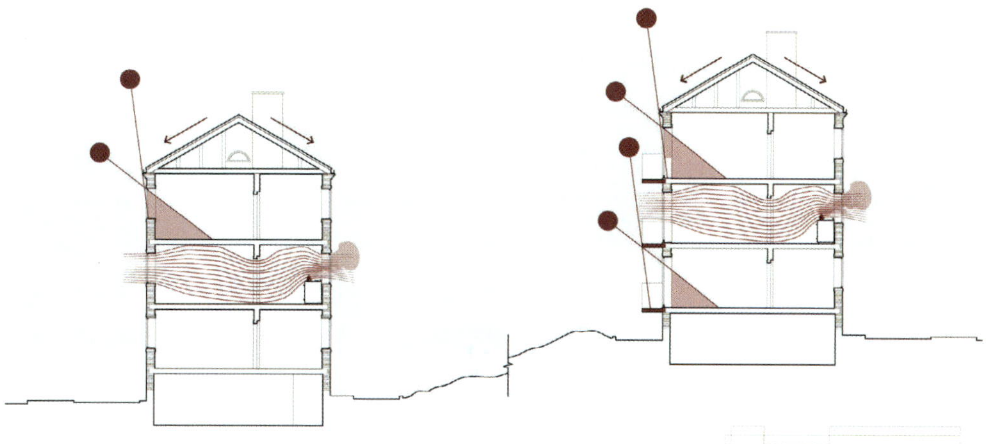

Floor plan with occupancy as originally designed

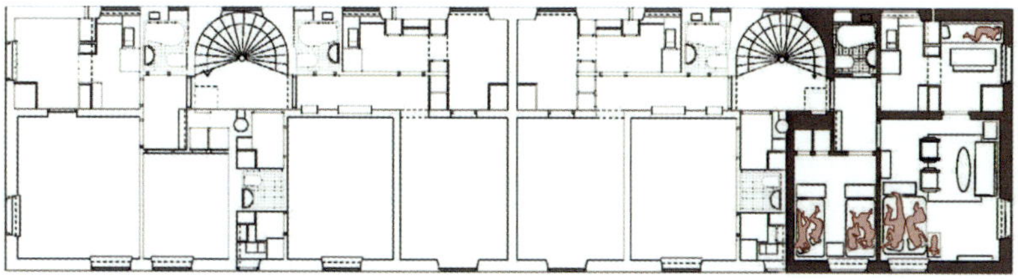

Plan with twenty-first-century occupancy

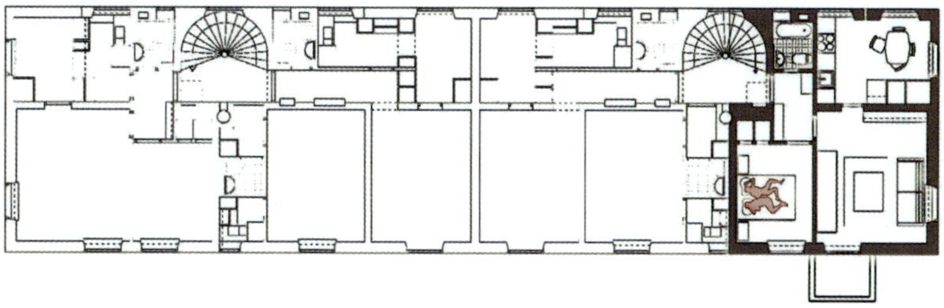

Hammarkullen
Angered, Gothenburg
1965–78

Bingyu He
and Jiaxing Yan

As part of the ambitious Swedish "Million Homes Programme" of the 1960s and '70s, publicly supported developments like Hammarkullen were designed as rapidly deployable, self-sufficient, and high-density housing to combat the shortage.[1] The Modernist structures and innovations, including the "longest European escalator," leading to a subterranean tram station, were a solution to an immediate problem but have been burdened by insufficient maintenance.[2] The resulting stigma surrounding such developments has been difficult to solve, although current renovations and government rehabilitation programs are making progress.[3]

1 Derek Rankine, "Sweden's Regeneration Challenge: The Million Homes Programme," surf.scot/swedens-regeneration-challenge-the-million-homes-programme.

2 Housing Evolutions, "Renovation without Rent Increases: The Hammarkullen Experience," housingevolutions.eu.

3 Housing Evolutions, "Renovation."

Experiments in Housing: Case Studies in Sweden

Hammarkullen region proximity to Gothenburg

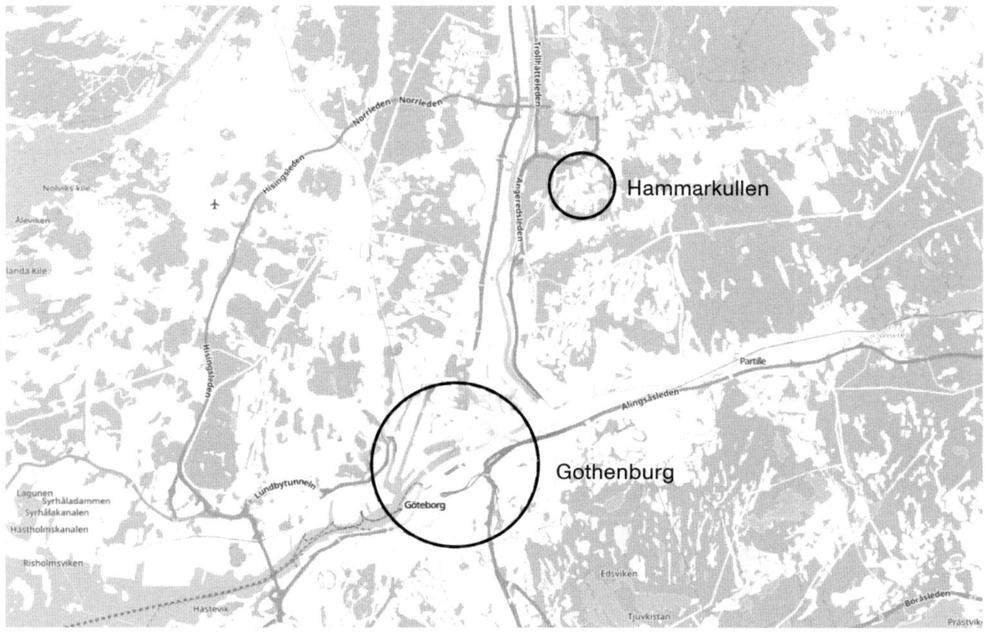

Development and growth between 1962 and 2003

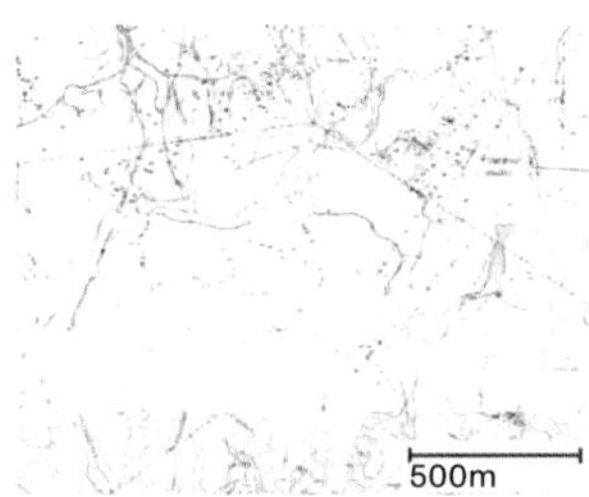

1962

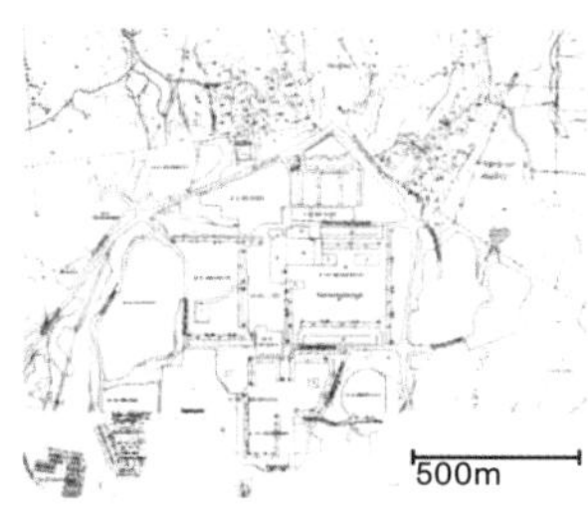

1969

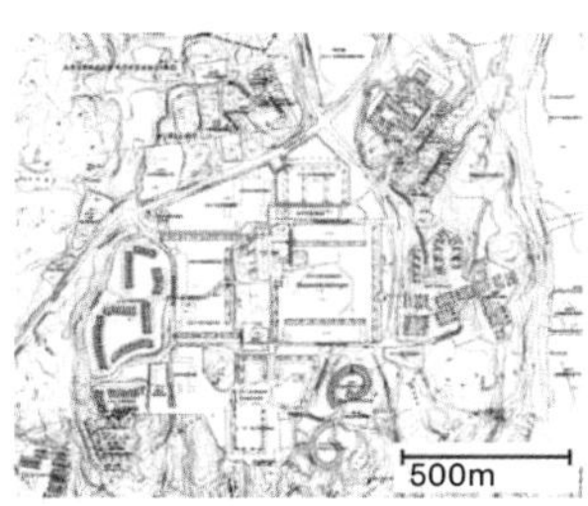

1982

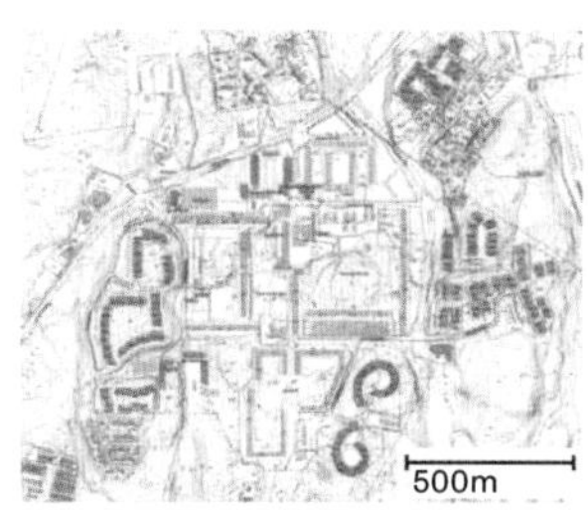

2003

Hammarkullen
Angered, Gothenburg
1965–78

Bingyu He
and Jiaxing Yan

Figure-ground study of buildings and green spaces in the Hammarkullen area

Extents of subsections by "walking area"

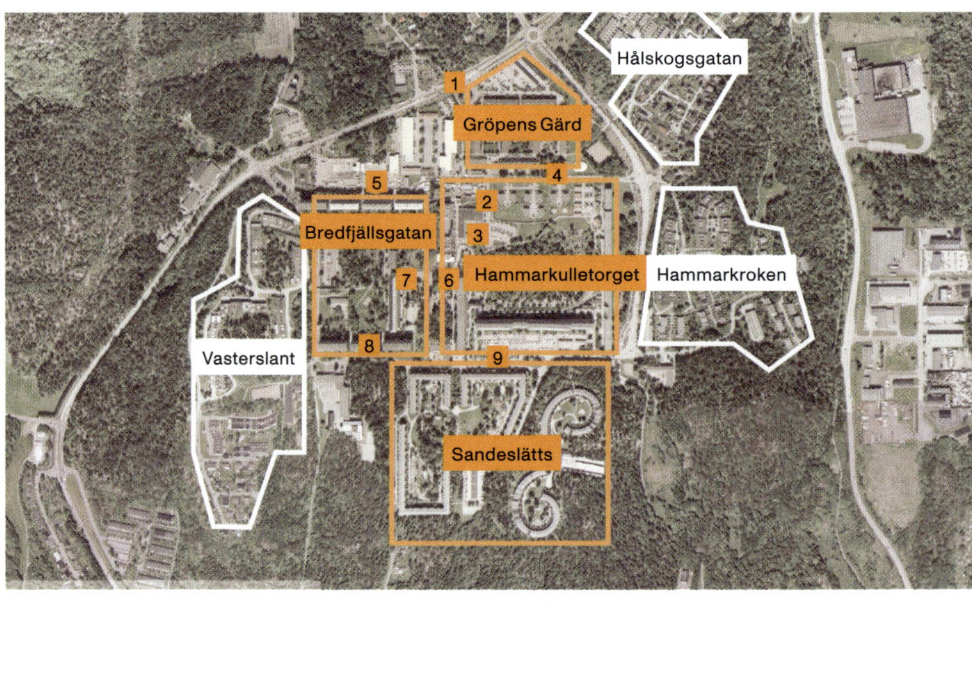

Verticality comparison: buildings within Hammarkullen vs. the Hammarkulletorget housing type

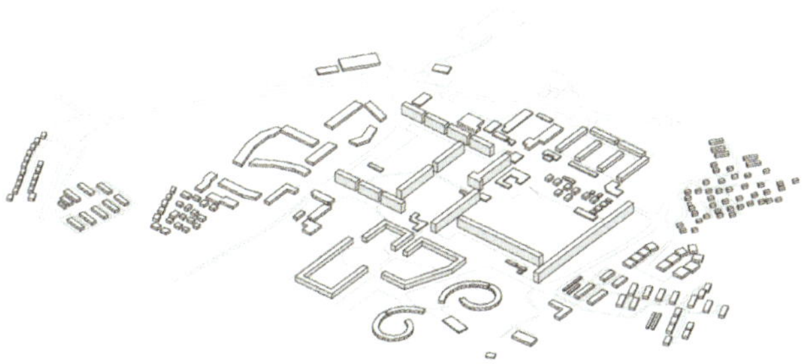

Elevation of Hammarkulletorget type as initially built

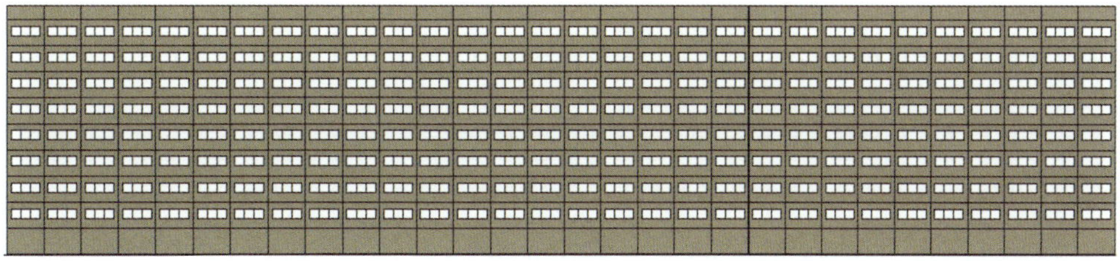

Views within the "walking area"

Typical floor plan

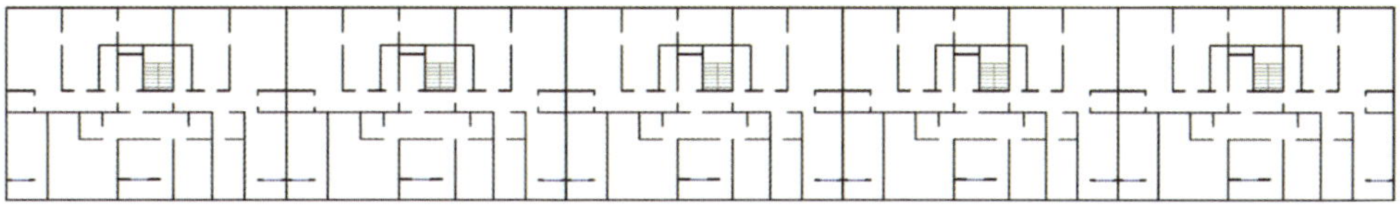

Bo01—Västra Hamnen, Malmö 1997–present

Andrea Sanchez Moctezuma and Jahaan Scipio

Sweden's Bo01 residential housing development project stands as a significant milestone in the country's sustainable urban design.[1] The transformation of the industrial shipyard on the southern coast combined principles of high-density living with sustainable development standards and incentives.[2] The "greenspace factor" guidelines, for instance, sought to promote better quality of life for residents based on a point system that maintained a site-wide average for ecological interventions that developers and architects made on each plot.[3]

1 Urban Green Blue Grids, "Bo01, Malmö, Sweden," urbangreenbluegrids.com.

2 De Natuurlijke Stad (The Natural City), "BO01 Västra Hamnen,"naturalcity.nl/2016/09/05/bo01-malmo.

3 De Natuurlijke Stad, "BO01 Västra Hamnen."

Malmö population as compared to Gothenburg and Stockholm

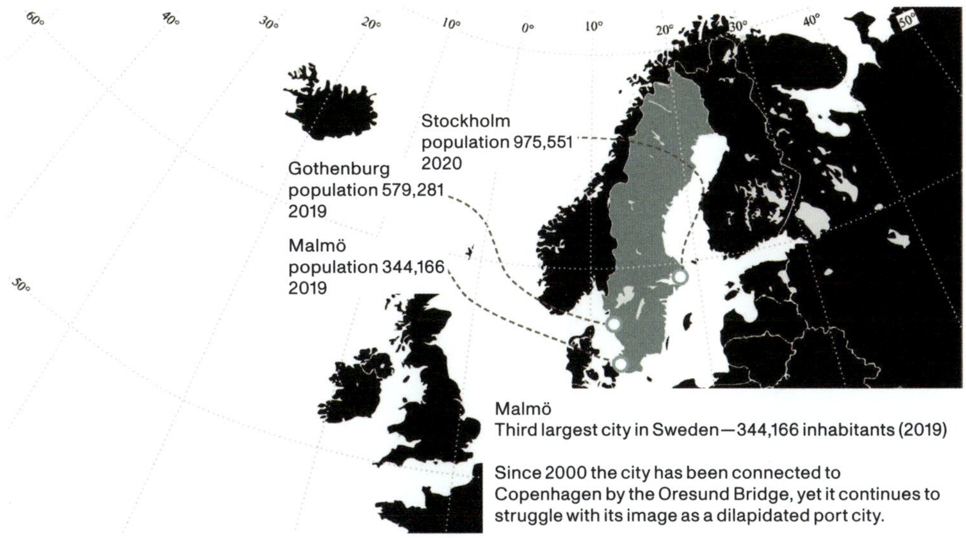

Malmö
Third largest city in Sweden—344,166 inhabitants (2019)

Since 2000 the city has been connected to Copenhagen by the Oresund Bridge, yet it continues to struggle with its image as a dilapidated port city.

Site relationship to public transit

Västra Hamnen, (western harbor) neighbourhood of Malmö, situated in the borough of Centrum, Malmö Municipality, Skåne County, Sweden

Bo01 is the first redevelopment of the post-industrial western harbor and began as an international housing exhibition in 2001.

Initiative:
The City of Malmö Local Investment Programme
The Swedish State
The European Union

Urban Planning & Master Plan
Klas Tham Design of Homes: 26 Architects

Bo01—Västra Hamnen, Malmö 1997–present

Andrea Sanchez Moctezuma and Jahaan Scipio

Bo01 site

Development figure-ground comparisons

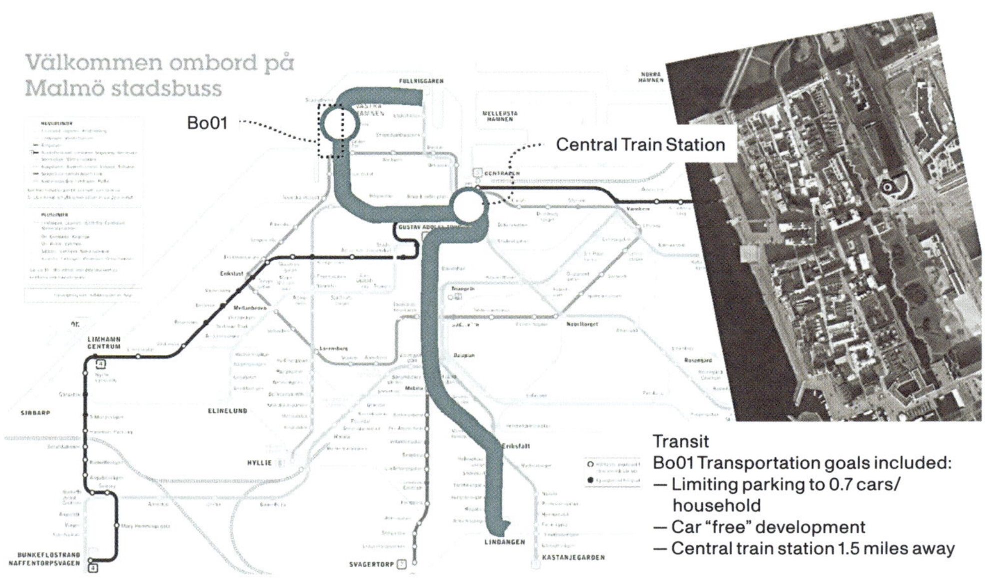

Transit
Bo01 Transportation goals included:
- Limiting parking to 0.7 cars/ household
- Car "free" development
- Central train station 1.5 miles away

Tango housing-unit arrangement around courtyard

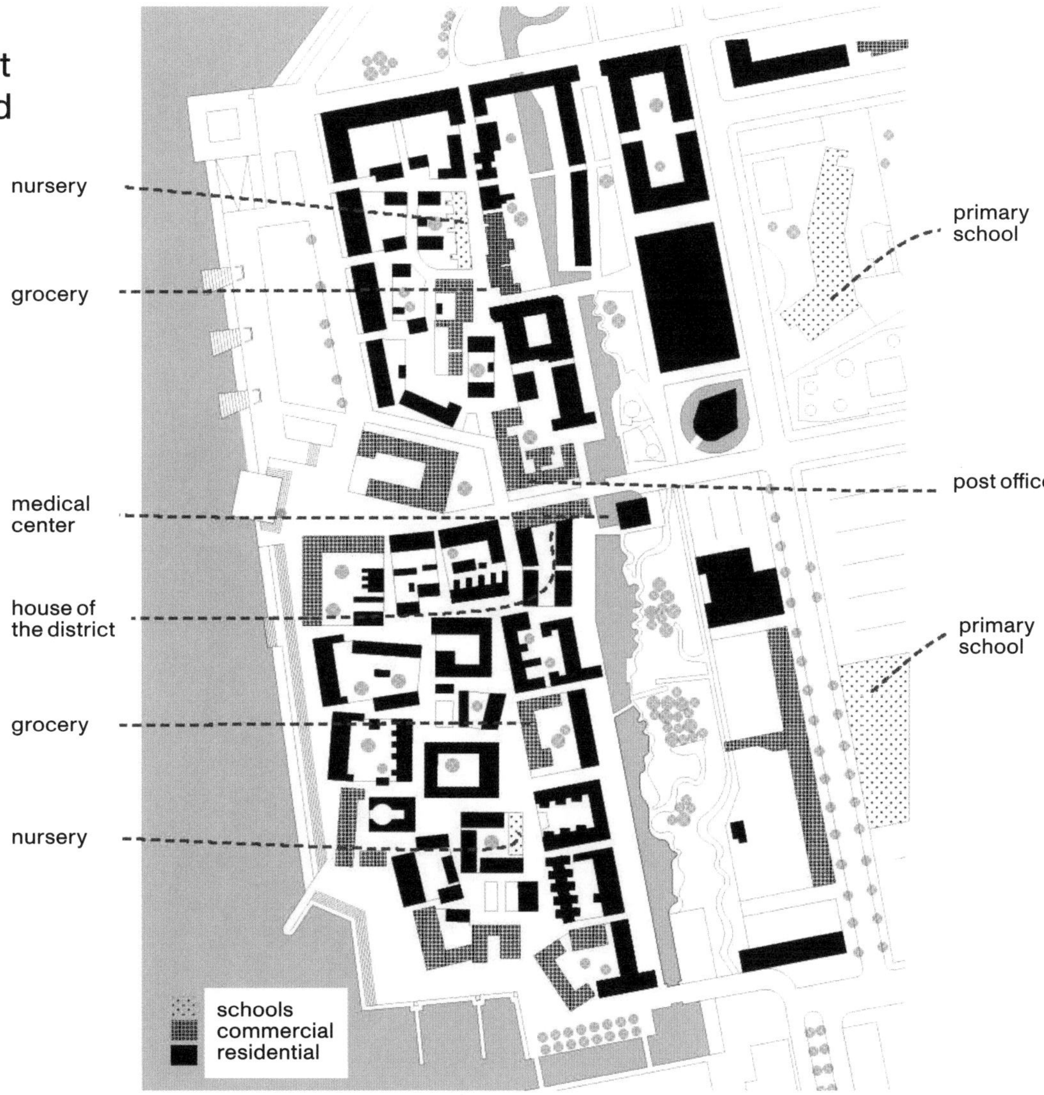

Bo01—Västra Hamnen, Malmö 1997–present

Andrea Sanchez Moctezuma and Jahaan Scipio

Amenity categorization

Water features and the sharing of space

Norra Djurgårdsstaden, Stockholm 2001–present

Bishrelt Solongo and Brent Wafula

Norra Djurgårdsstaden, one of Stockholm's largest industrial zones in the nineteenth century, has undergone dramatic urban development as the Stockholm Royal Seaport.[1] Through infrastructural, sustainable, and social policies connected to its unified development vision, the 236-hectare project is now one of Europe's largest urban-development projects, with 12,000 new homes and 35,000 workplaces.[2]

1 Stockholms Stad, "Stockholm Royal Seaport," vaxer.stockholm/en/areas/city-development-areas/stockholm-royal-seaport.

2 IVL Swedish Environmental Research Institute, "Stormwater Management Makes Stockholm Royal Seaport a Resilient Model," smartcitysweden.com/best-practice/362/let-the-nature-do-the-work-stockholm-royal-seaport.

Norra Djurgårdsstaden location scale and population size

Sweden

Population
10,234,240

Provinces
25

Area
450,295 km^2

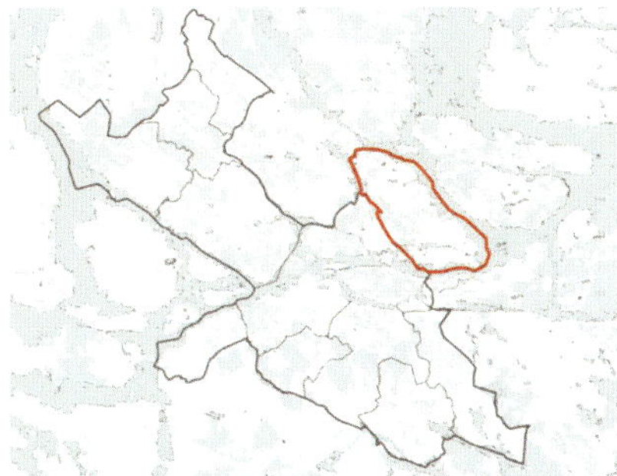

Stockholm

Population
1,679,000

Provinces
14

Area
381.63 km^2

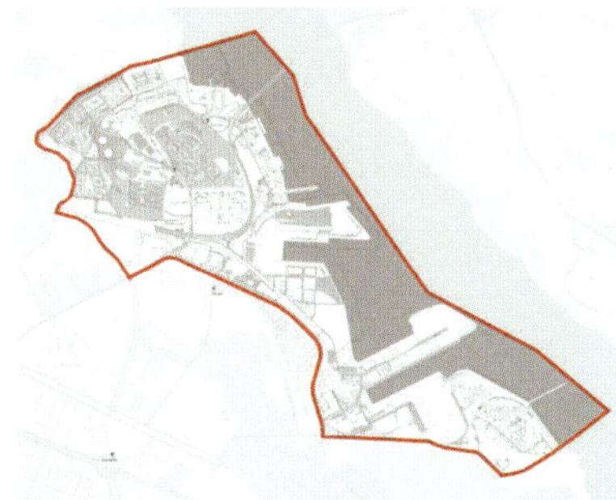

Norra Djurgardsstaden in Ostermalm

Population
71,802

Area
18 km^2

Photographic timeline of Hjorthagen's major industries

1853

1879–1886

1882

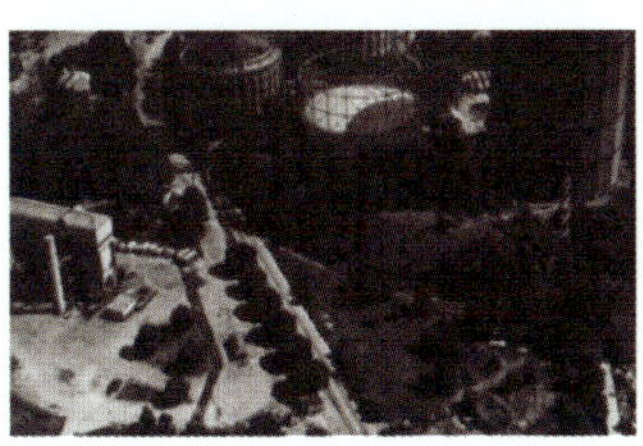

1893

1903

1904

Norra Djurgårdsstaden, Stockholm 2001–present

Bishrelt Solongo and Brent Wafula

Completed recent development

Stockholm Royal Seaport development metrics and housing data

236 hectares	Stockholm Royal Seaport is half the size of Sodermalm and comprises the subareas Hjorthagen, Vartahamnen, Frihamnen, and Loudden.
12,000	At least 12,000 new housing units have been planned, most of them along Husarviken in Hjorthagen, and on Loudden. Occupation of the Garphyttan block in Hjothagen began in October 2012.
35,000	New workplaces are planned. Occupaton of the Riga block in Sodra Vartahamnen began in 2010.
600,000 m²	of commercial floor space is planned.
52%	of the apartments in Stockholm Royal Seaport are rental apartments.
48%	are tenant-owned apartments.
8%	of the rental apartments are students accommodation.
20%	to date of commercial space accounted for.

Figure-ground study of project structures

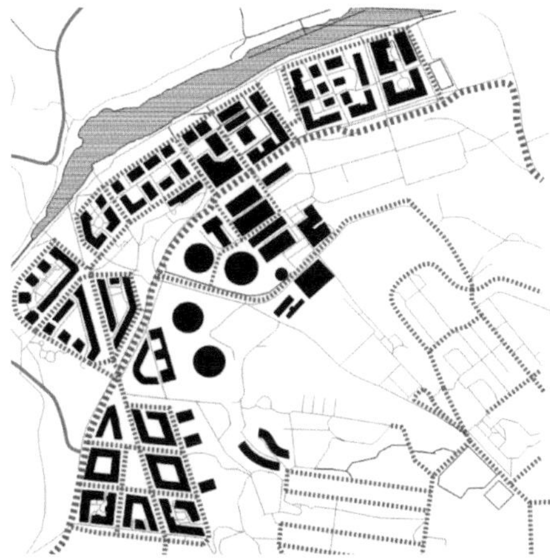

Culturally significant structures remaining in the development

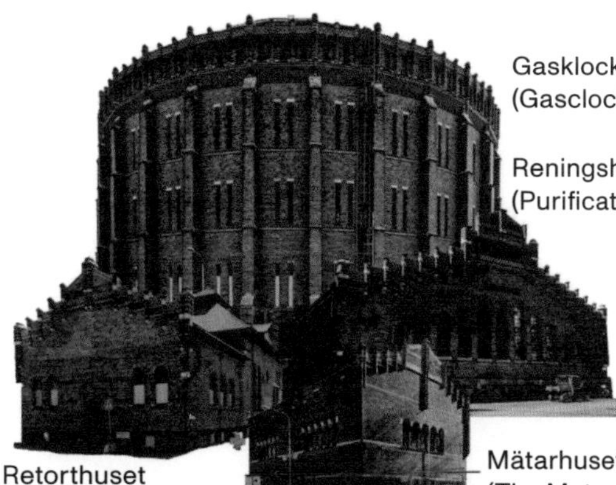

Materiality and textures of Norra Djurgårdsstaden

Vallastaden, Linköping 2001–present

Maxwell Baum and Zishi Li

Beginning in 2012 and showcased in 2017, Vallastaden's unique approach to urban planning featured housing with diverse ownership types, requirements for renewable construction materials, alternative energy models, and groundbreaking infrastructure design practice.[1] The project stemmed from a bottom-up approach, first conceptualized in a competition then enacted by 40 planning stakeholders.[2] They implemented "quality-based" criteria for land sales, which encouraged developers to fully realize sustainable systems in their interventions.[3] What resulted from this policy was a cross-sectoral urban plan that connected and incentivized the development of transportation, local businesses, housing, and energy.[4]

1 Nordregio, "Vallastaden: A Diverse, Bottom-up Housing Development," nordregio.org/sustainable_cities/vallastaden.

2 Nordregio, "Vallastaden."sustainable_cities/vallastaden.

3 Cleantech Östergötland, "Vallastaden: A Model for Sustainable Planning of Cities and Districts," smartcitysweden.com/best-practice/352/vallastaden-a-model-for-sustainable-planning-of-cities-and-districts.

4 Cleantech Östergötland, "Vallastaden."

Transit proximity to Linköping

Vallastaden proximity to university campus and science park in Linköping

Vallastaden, Linköping 2012–present

Maxwell Baum and Zishi Li

Underground culvert system

Figure-ground study: buildable area 76,800 m² vs. built area 38,965 m²

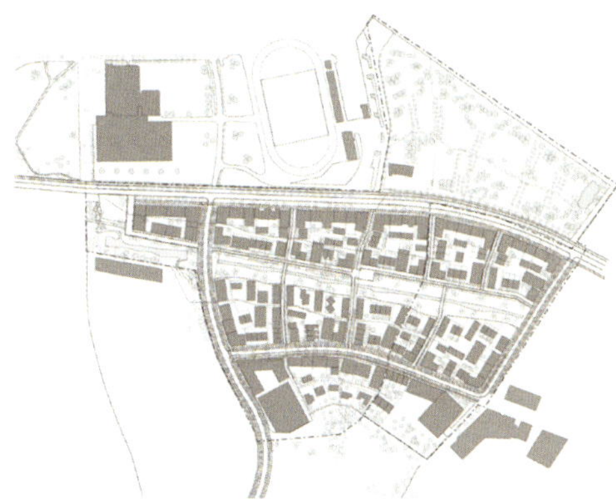

Built/unbuilt areas as of 2022

Built and planned community greenhouses as of 2022

Shared public space

Strategic positioning of high-density buildings to roadways and interior pedestrian walkways

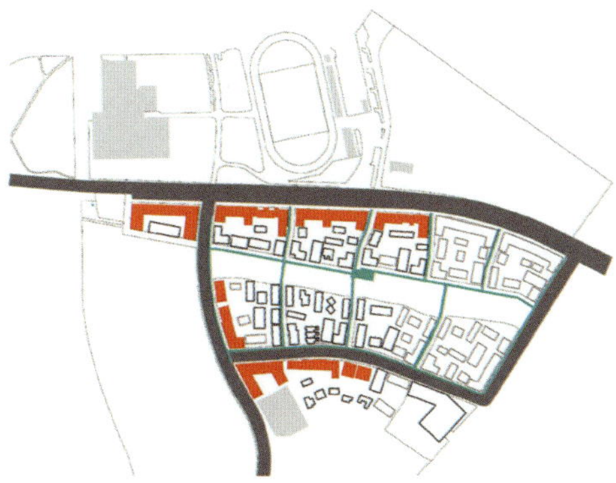

Vallastaden, Linköping 2012–present

Maxwell Baum and Zishi Li

High-density buildings equaling 59.5% of total development gross floor area

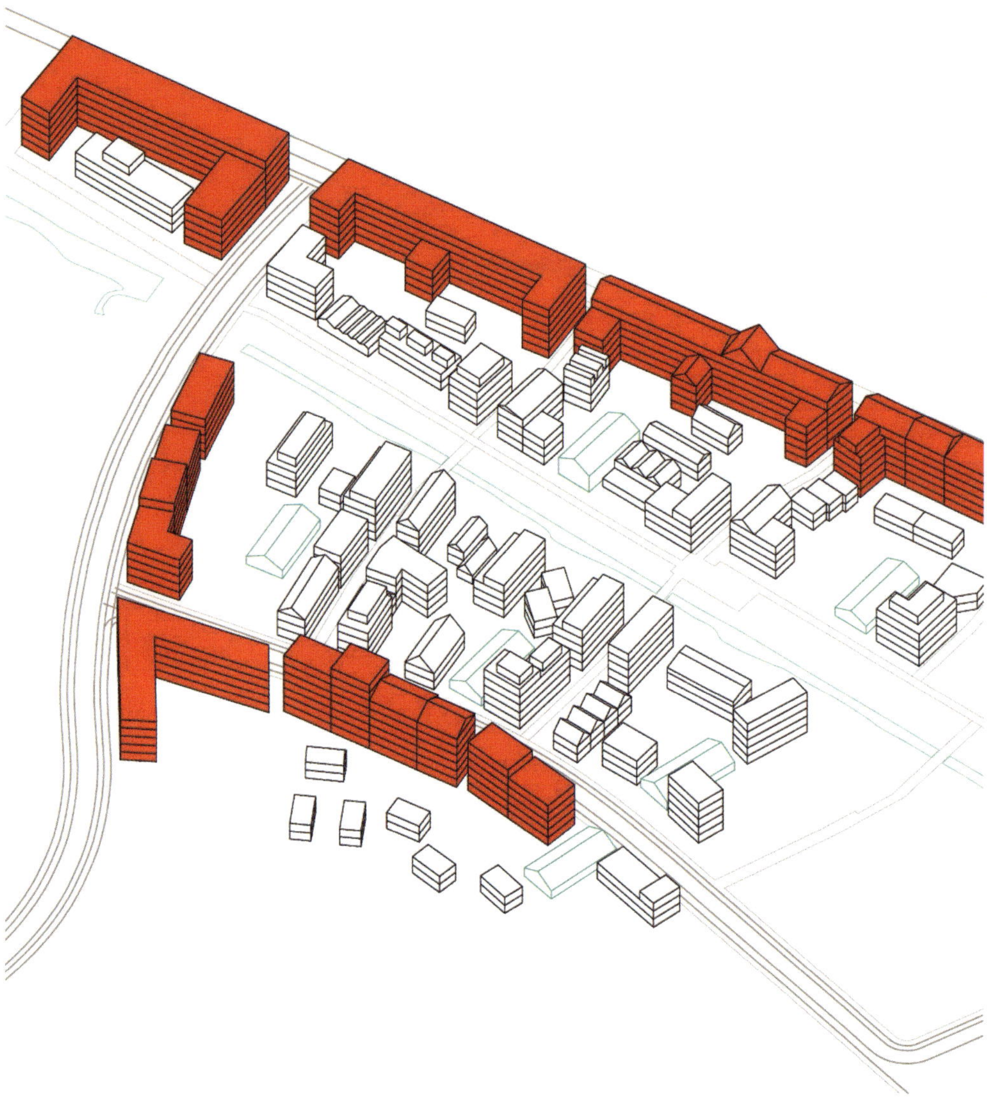

Experiments in Housing: Case Studies in Canada

While the first research assignment centered on the urban scale of successful communities in Sweden, the second narrowed the investigative focus to the building scale within the Canadian context of Toronto. Continuing research in pairs, two groups took on the larger scale and multiphase adaptive reuse of Regent Park, and the remaining pairs selected stand-alone developments from the 1970s and '80s. The illustrative investigations demonstrated the performative standards and expectations of the housing developments and how this was accomplished through their design.

Sackville Place Millington Street, Cabbagetown 1700s–present

Bishrelt Solongo and Brent Wafula

In the mid-nineteenth century, the Irish immigrant neighborhood Cabbagetown saw significant urban growth.[1] Amid the rapid industrial development of railways in Toronto, the area became known for its stately Victorian-style homes.[2] Millington Street has remained notable for this architecture and was the subject of restoration efforts in the 1970s to preserve the historic character of the neighborhood.[3]

1 Cabbagetown BIA, cabbagetownto.com.

2 J.M.S. Careless, "The Emergence of Cabbagetown in Victorian Toronto," archives.studentscommission.ca/magic/mt37.html.

3 History of Toronto, "Cabbagetown Toronto: Exploring the Historic and Vibrant Neighborhood," historyoftoronto.ca/blog/cabbagetown-toronto-exploring-the-historic-and-vibrant-neighborhood#google_vignette.

Millington Street in 1858 and its relation to the existing Winchester and Parliament Streets

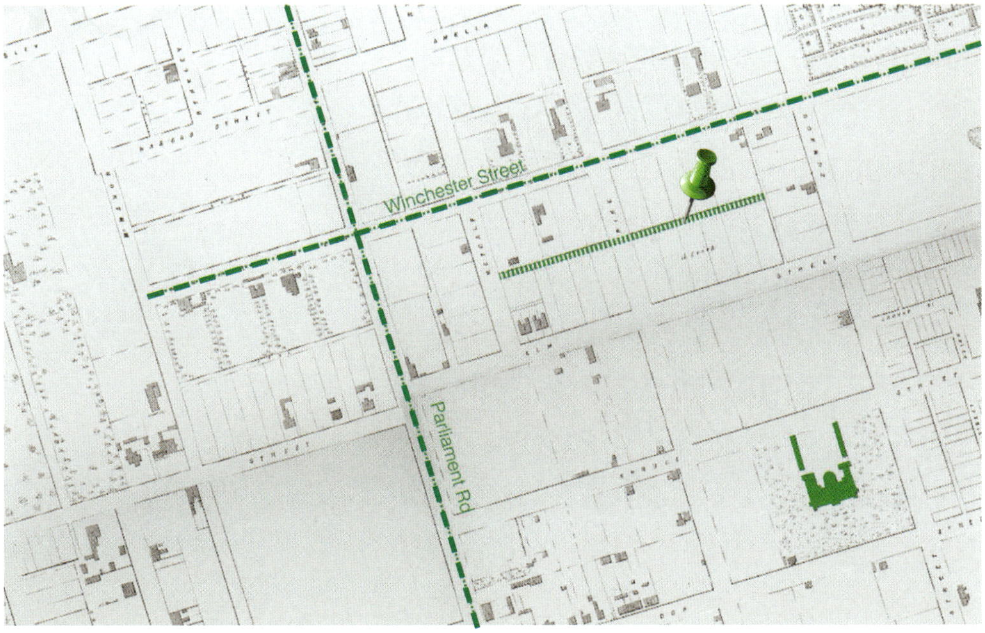

Millington Street in 1903

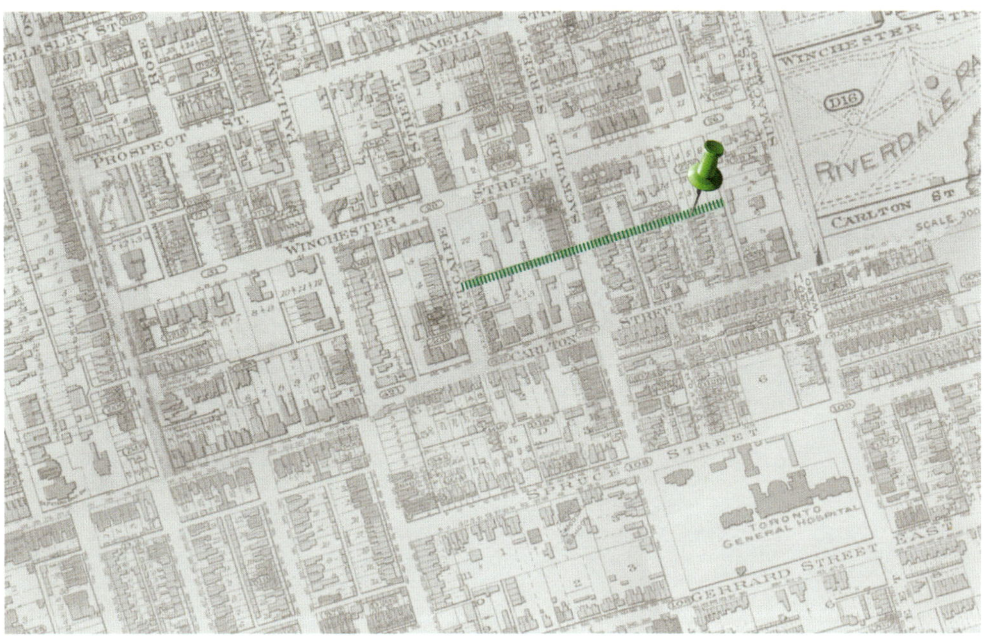

Sackville Place Millington Street, Cabbagetown 1700s–present

Bishrelt Solongo and Brent Wafula

Millington Street in 1924

Millington Street as of 2022

Public transit along Parliament Street near Millington Street

Sackville Place Millington Street, Cabbagetown 1700s–present

Bishrelt Solongo and Brent Wafula

Green space and park infrastructure near Millington and Parliament Streets in Cabbagetown

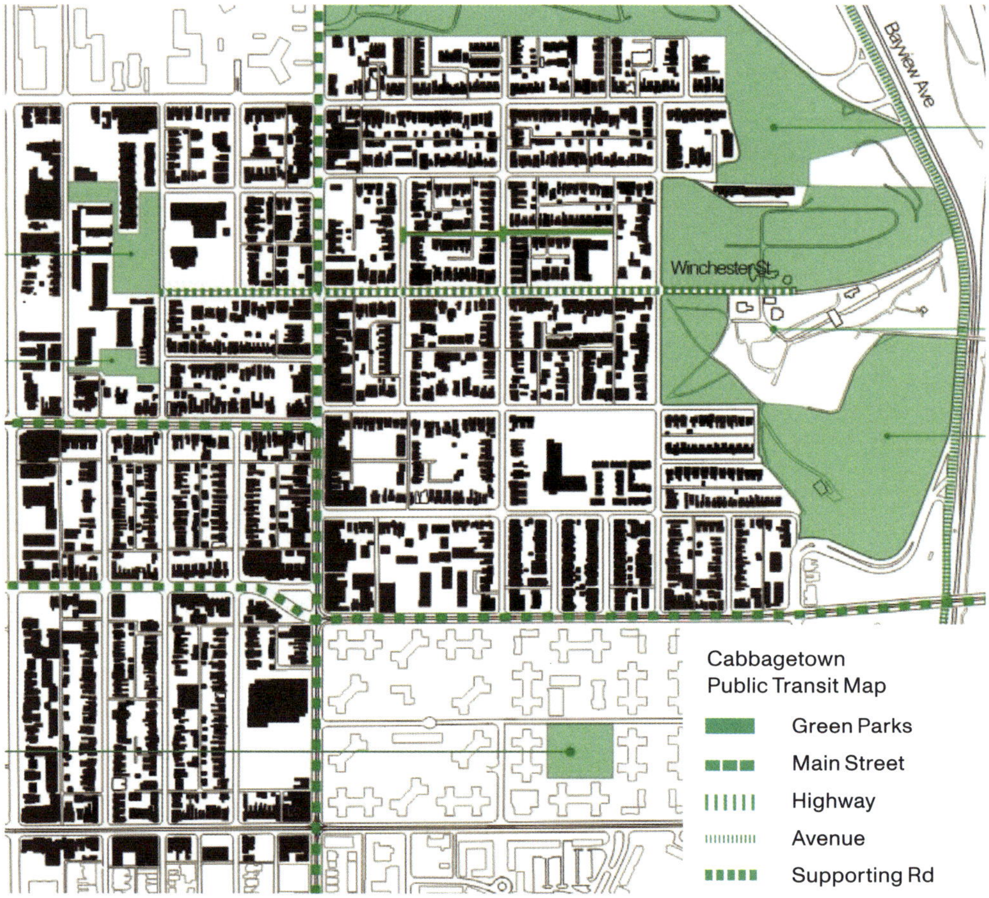

Public programs near and around Millington and Parliament Streets

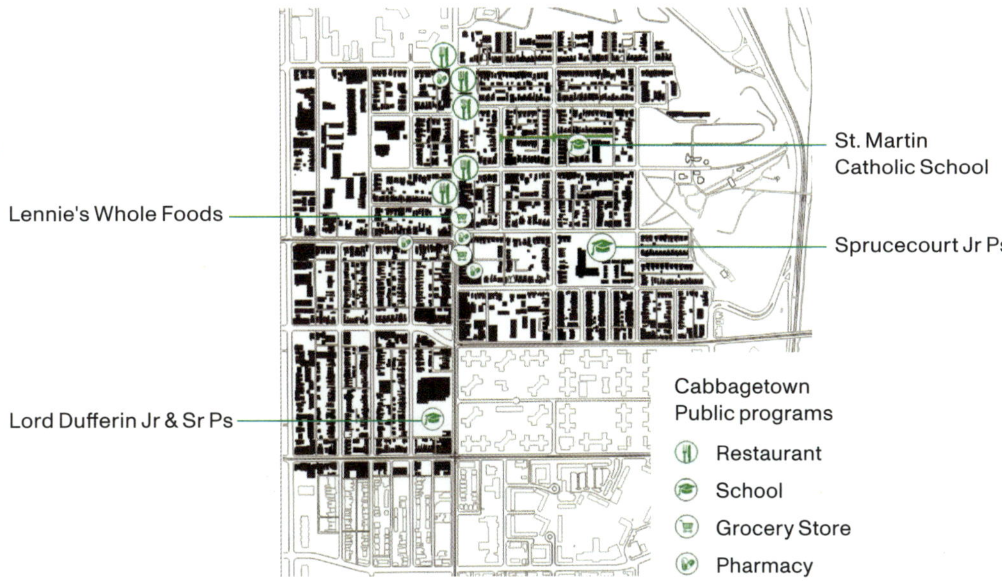

Variety of development and developers along Millington and Parliament Streets in Cabbagetown

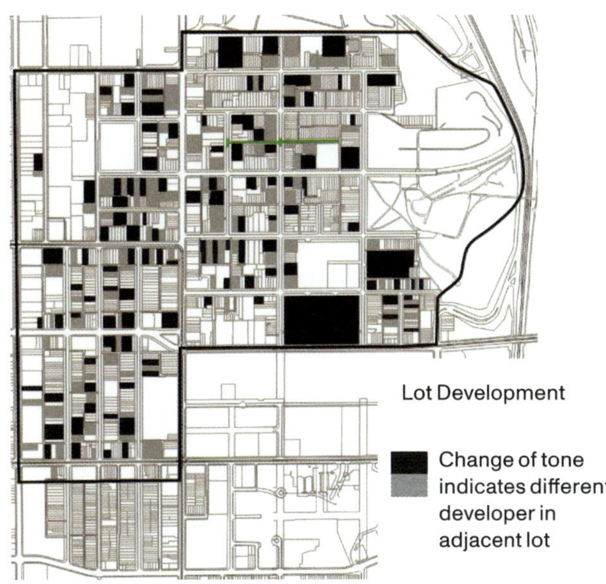

The Esplanade, St. Lawrence Neighborhood 1850s–present

Bingyu He
and Jiaxing Yan

The Esplanade has defined the edge of Toronto's downtown since its inception. In the 1850s it was established as the path for railways between the artificially constructed and natural land masses along the emerging industrial waterfront.[1] Recent transformations have sought to repair the negative community impacts of the twentieth-century highway developments, yielding a chain of public parks and pedestrian walkways.

1 History of Toronto, "Cabbagetown".

View of Toronto in 1854

Map of Toronto Harbour, formerly known as York Harbour, in 1793 (courtesy of Toronto Public Library)

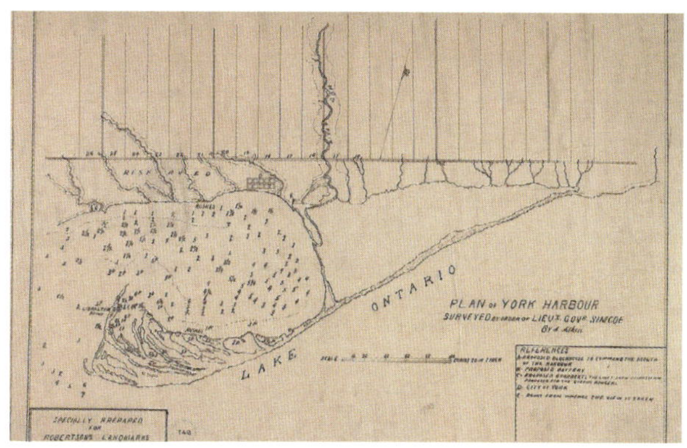

Outline of harbor edge from 1818 overlaid on 2022 map

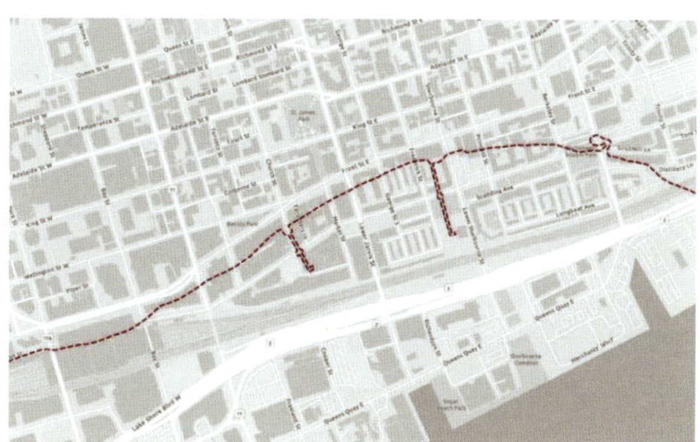

The Esplanade, St. Lawrence Neighborhood 1850s–present

Bingyu He and Jiaxing Yan

The Esplanade and 2022 harbor edge

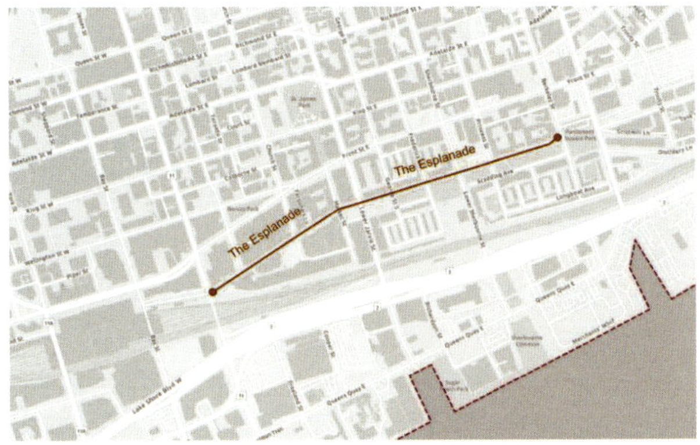

Figure-ground study of structures along the Esplanade

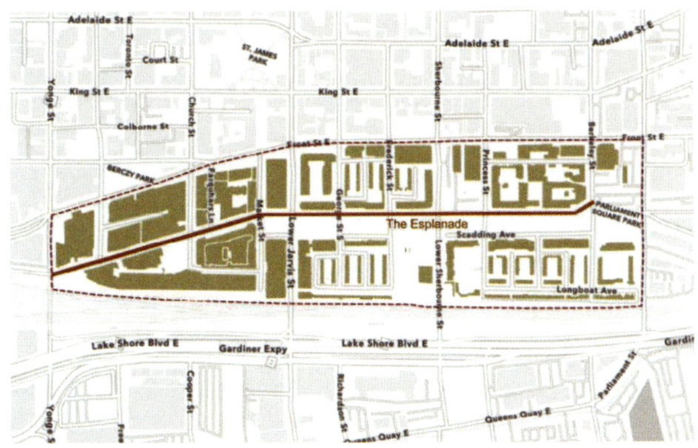

Adjacent major rail-transit corridors

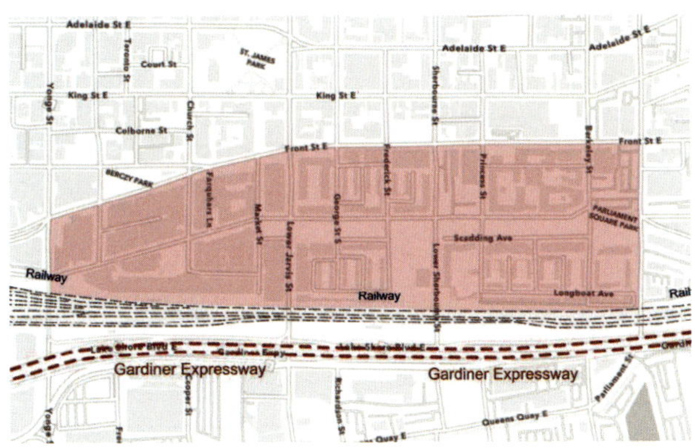

High-rise building scale comparison surrounding The Esplanade

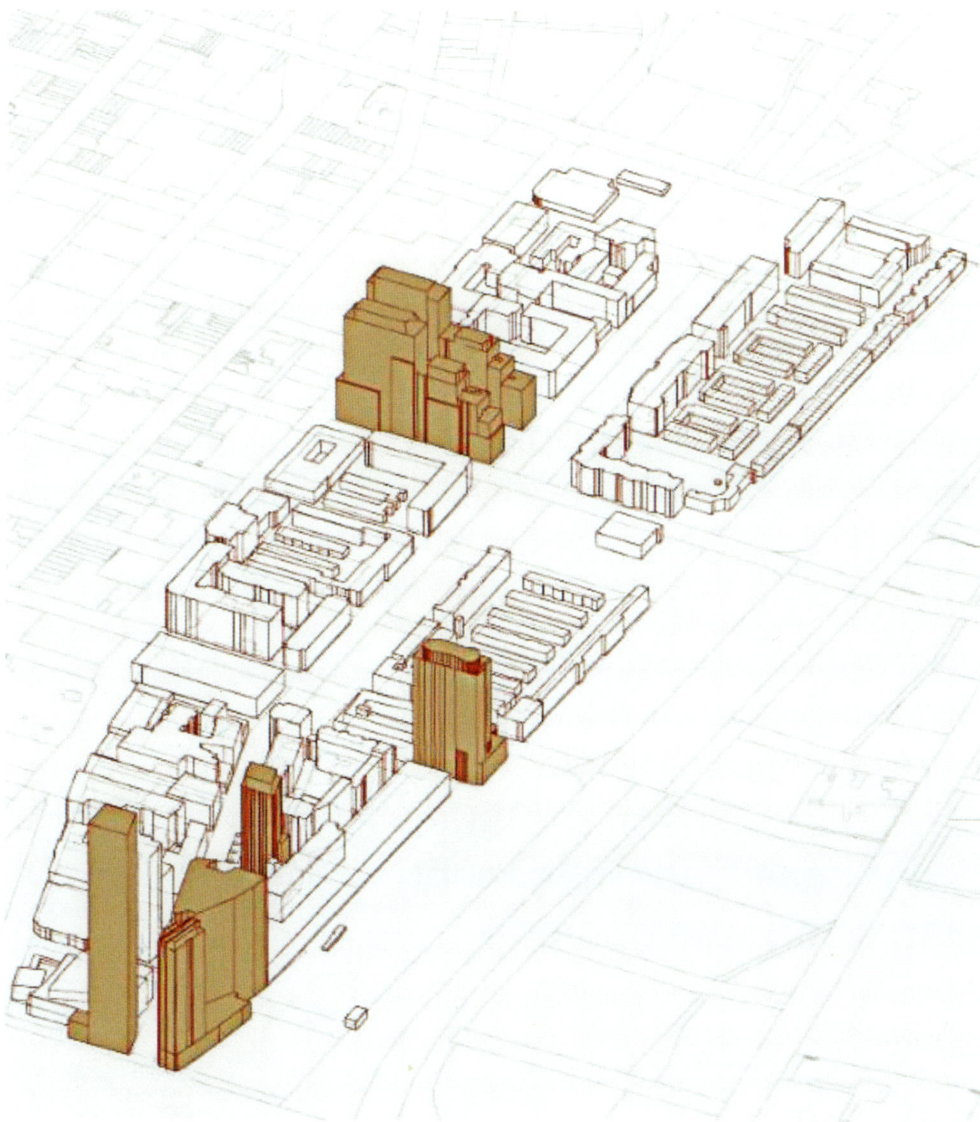

Regent Park, Toronto 1850s–present

Noah Sannes and Charis Armstrong

Originally part of the Cabbagetown neighborhood, Regent Park is a long-standing public housing development that has evolved in scope and public perception since its construction in 1940.[1] In the 1970s public complaints about the deterioration of the development and possible city government responses were discussed, but action was limited.[2] In response to public advocacy in the mid-1990s, a four-phase redevelopment plan was implemented in 2005 with the aim of creating a mixed-income, mixed-use community with modern amenities by 2030.[3]

1 Urbaneer.com, "Garden City: The History and Revitalization of Toronto's Regent Park Neighbourhood."

2 Cabbagetowninfo.com, "How Regent Park Became One of the World's Largest Redevelopments," cabbagetowninfo.com/how-regent-park-became-one-of-the-worlds-largest-redevelopments.

3 Urban Park, "Regent Park," urbanplan.uli.org/resources/overview/project-snapshots/regent-park.

Toronto's Regent Park Neighborhood

Facade of three-story apartment building

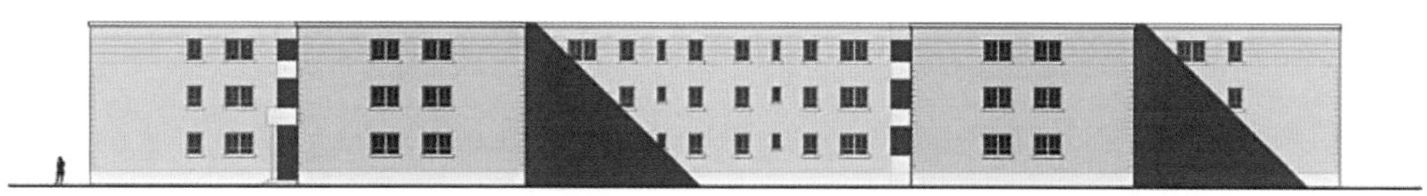

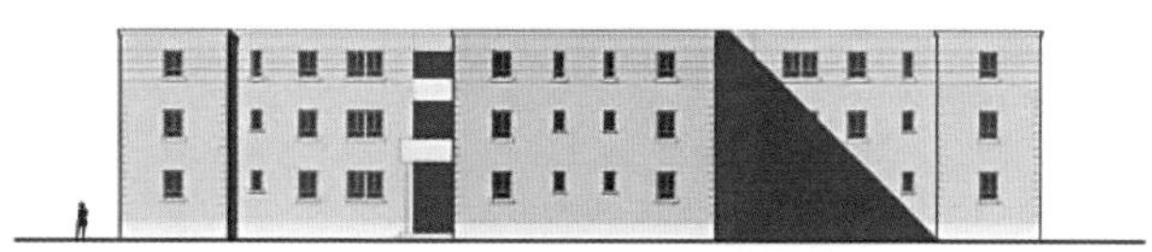

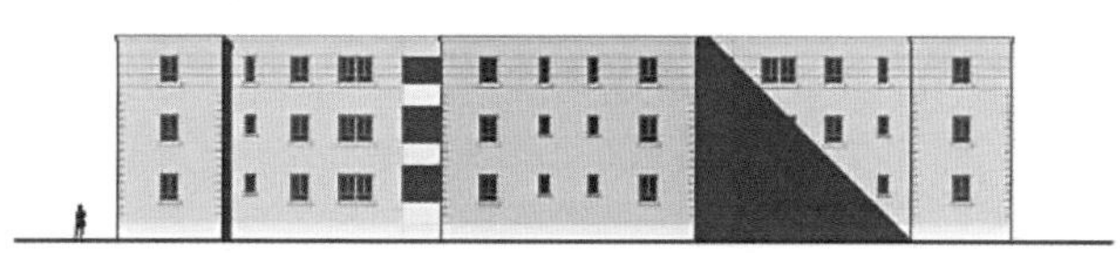

Regent Park, Toronto 1930s–present

Noah Sannes
and Charis Armstrong

Phases of development, Regent Park North (1950)

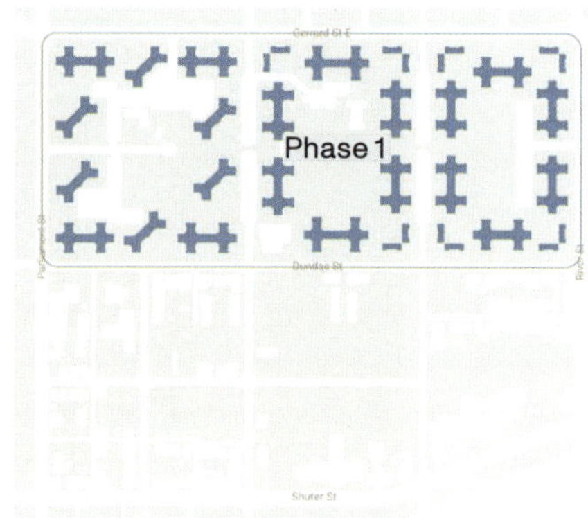

Phases of development: South Regent Park (1960)

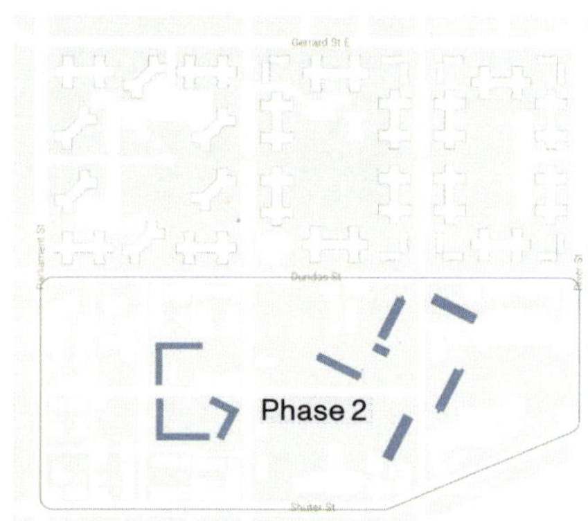

Figure-ground study, built structure

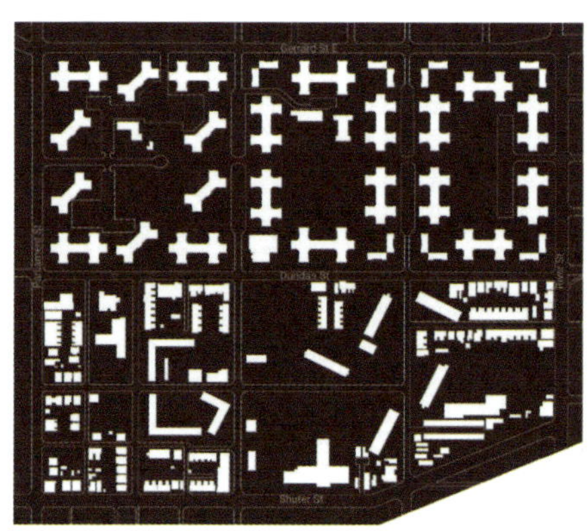

Typical floor plan of three-story apartment building

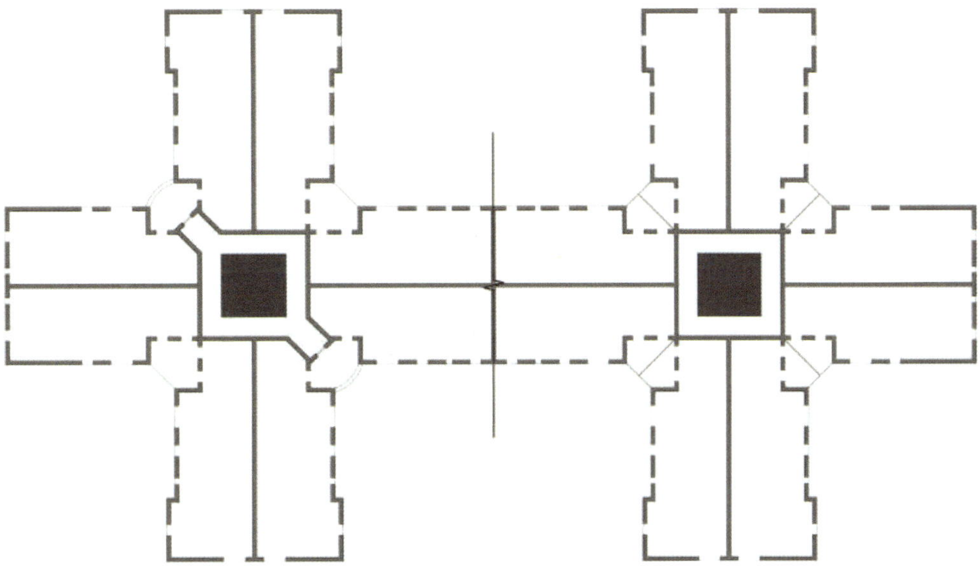

Five phases of redevelopment plan as of 2022

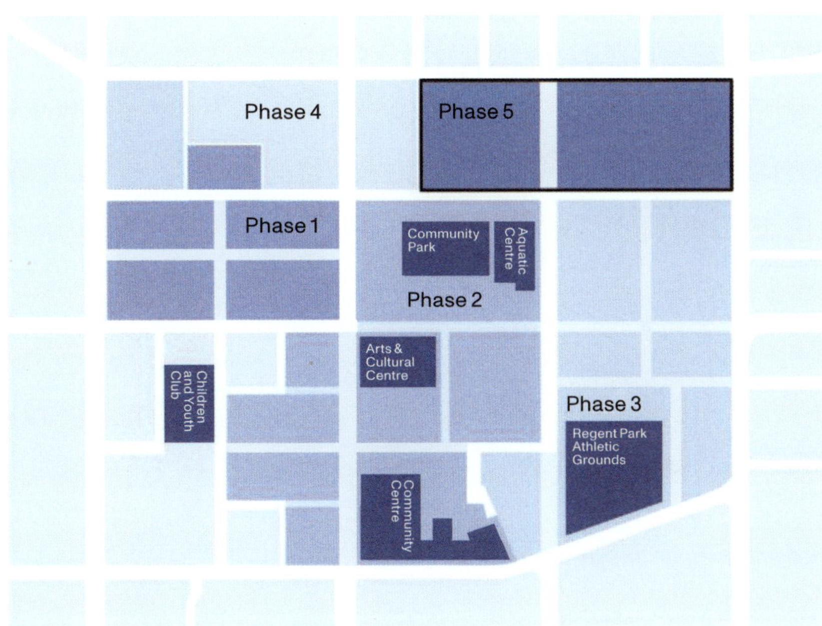

Bain Co-op, Cabbagetown 1960s–present

Andrea Sanchez Moctezuma and Jahaan Scipio

Built by Toronto Housing Authority in 1913 and originally known as the Riverdale Courts, the Bain Co-op Housing Development was one of the first social housing projects in Canada to be influenced by the English Garden City Movement.[1] By 1974 the property was home to a diverse community and was facing a potential conversion to condominiums due to physical deterioration.[2] The tenants organized and transformed the property into a housing cooperative by 1977, assuring that it is democratically run and progressing toward completion of the mortgage while fostering a close-knit community.[3]

1 Bainco-op.ca, "Bain Co-op History," bainco-op.ca/our-history/?form=MG0AV3.

2 Bainco-op.ca, "Bain Co-op History."

3 Bainco-op.ca, "Bain Co-op History."

Comparison of Toronto and Edmonton populations to Stockholm, Gothenburg, and Malmö

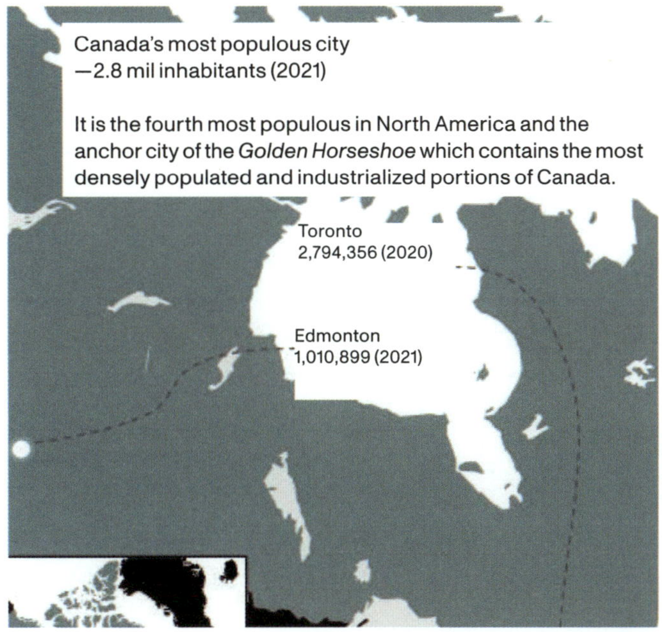

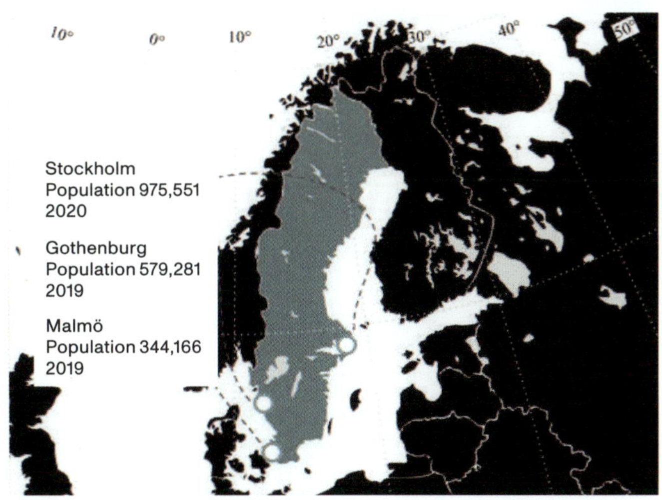

Malmö is the third largest city in Sweden
—344,166 inhabitants (2019)

Since 2000 the city has been connected to Copenhagen by the Oresund Bridge, yet it continued to struggle with its image as a dilapidated port city.

Bain Co-op, Cabbagetown 1960s–present

Andrea Sanchez Moctezuma and Jahaan Scipio

Typical floor plans: one-bedroom and one-bedroom with dining room

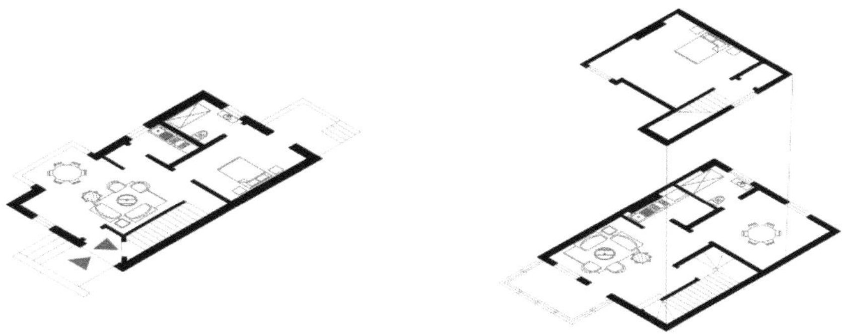

Typical floor plans: two-bedroom and two-bedroom with dining room

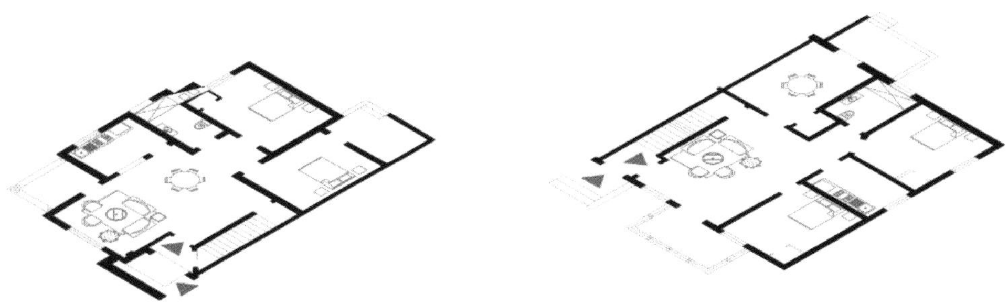

Typical floor plans: three-bedroom and three-bedroom with dining room

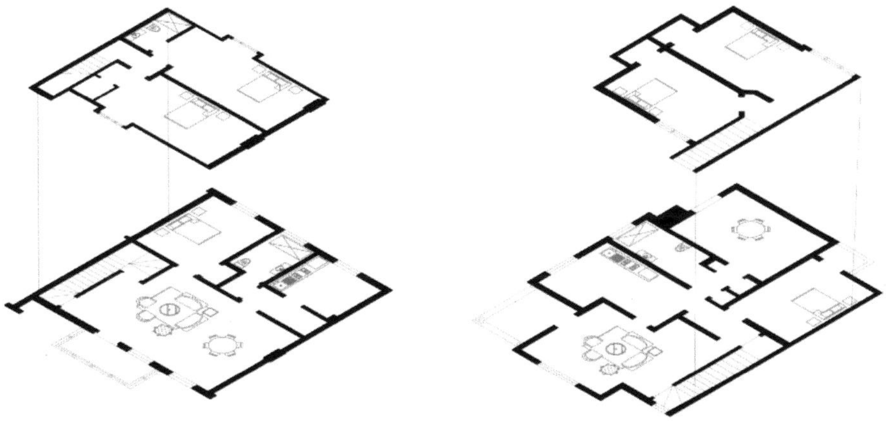

Typical floor plans: four-bedroom and two-bedroom town house

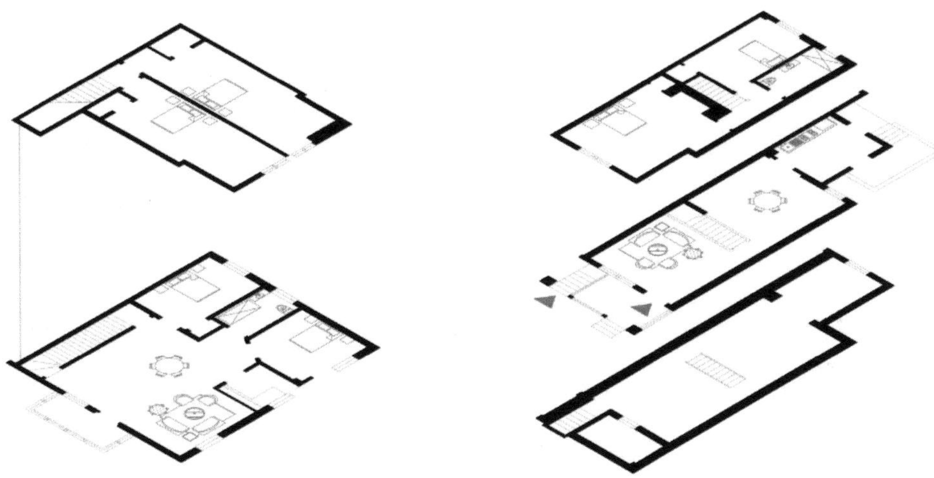

Bain Co-op, Cabbagetown 1960s–present

Andrea Sanchez Moctezuma and Jahaan Scipio

Facade character of the Bain Co-op

Green space and important landmarks near Bain Co-op

Shared and nonshared spaces in relation to general circulation

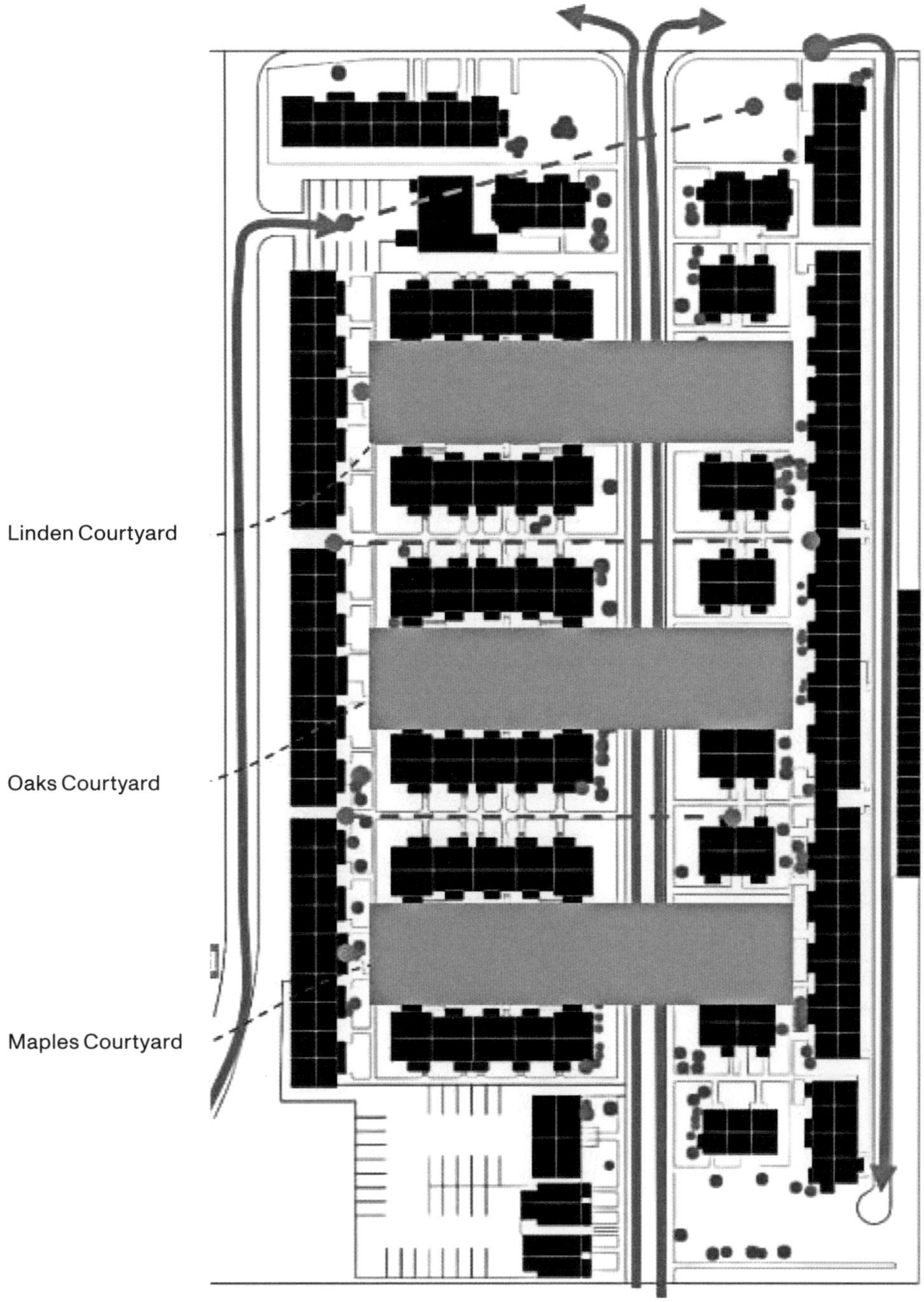

King's Landing, Toronto 1980s–present

Maxwell Baum and Zishi Li

King's Landing proximity to Billy Bishop Airport transit access

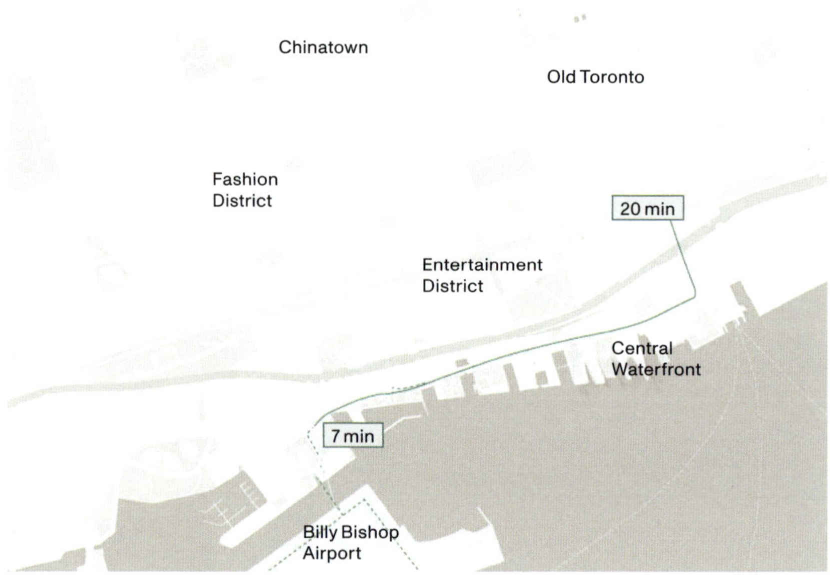

Front Street presents a reminder of how much land has been reclaimed over the years since it lies roughly along the original coastline

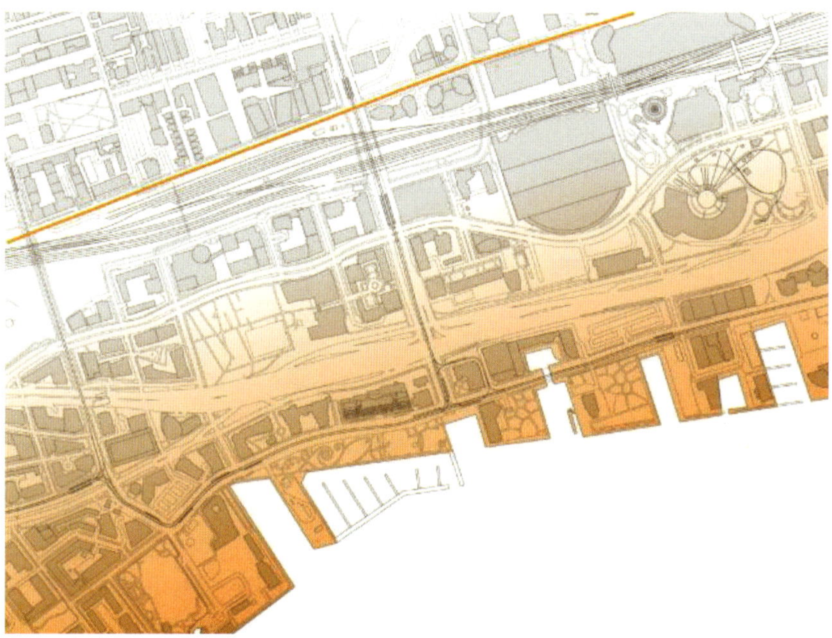

Area of apartment and condo buildings

King's Landing in relation to major transit and rail corridors

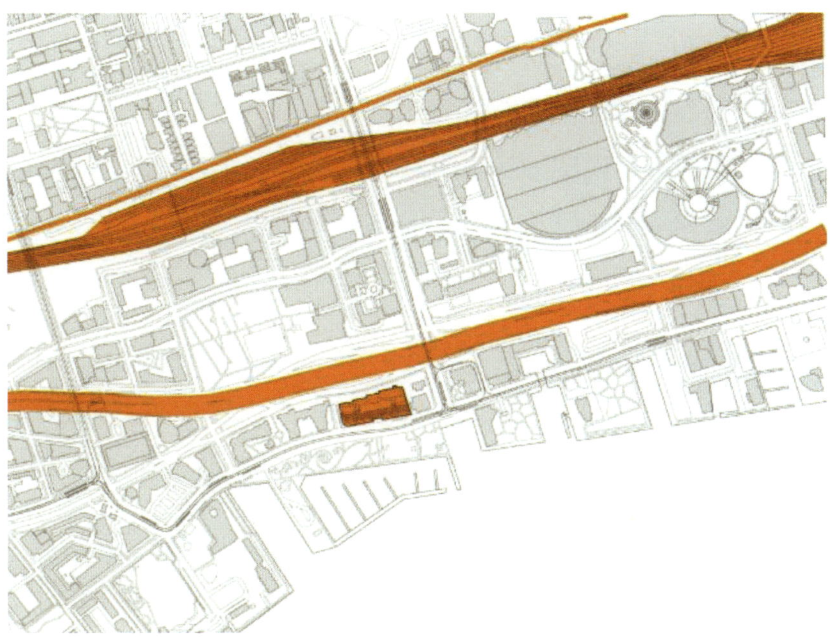

King's Landing, Toronto 1980s–present

Maxwell Baum and Zishi Li

The King's Landing development was the product of the 1985 Toronto Waterfront Competition, which aimed to revitalize the formerly industrial corridor.[1] The winning design, by architect Arthur Erickson, employed a series of stepped terraces to maximize views toward Lake Ontario and connect to public parks and mixed-use venues along the waterfront.[2] Since its construction in 1988, King's Landing has continued to attract public and private investment in its restoration efforts, transforming one of the most prominent confluences of the urban environment and nature in Toronto.[3]

1 Canadian Centre for Architecture, cca.qc.ca/en/archives/108951/fonds-arthur-erickson/397577/architectural-projects/414530/kings-landing-harbourfront-toronto-ontario?form=MG0AV3.

2 Canadian Centre for Architecture.

3 Architectural Conservancy of Ontario, "King's Landing," acotoronto.ca/building.php?ID=1335&form=MG0AV3.

Aerial view of Toronto's shoreline in 1918 and 1890 map from the Atlas of the City of Toronto (courtesy of Toronto Public Library)

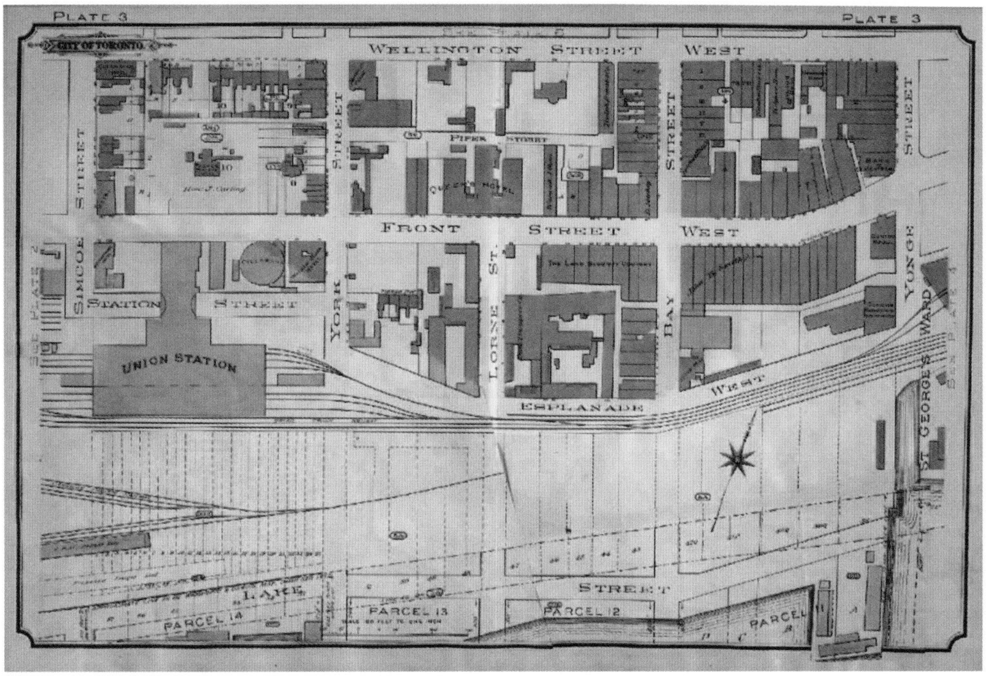

King's Landing, Toronto 1980s–present

Maxwell Baum and Zishi Li

Underground parking for residents, customers, and visitors to the National Ballet Centre

King's Landing site before and during construction

Tram transit lines in relation to King's Landing

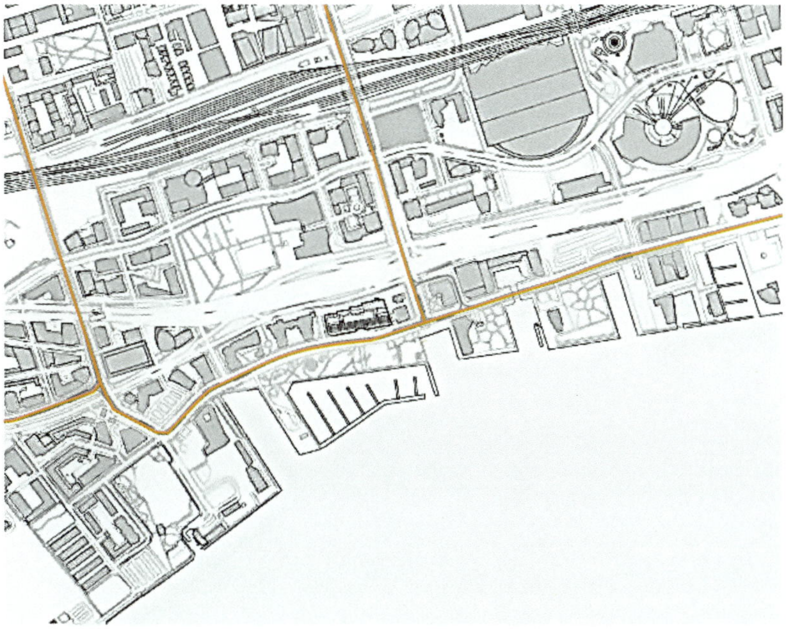

Comparison of development density and lot coverage between Vallastaden and King's Landing

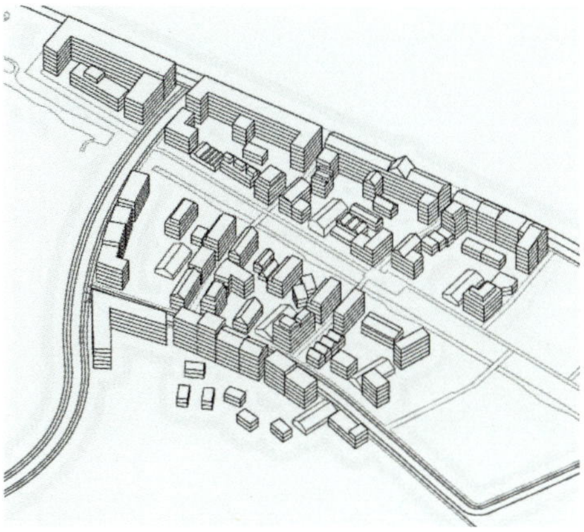

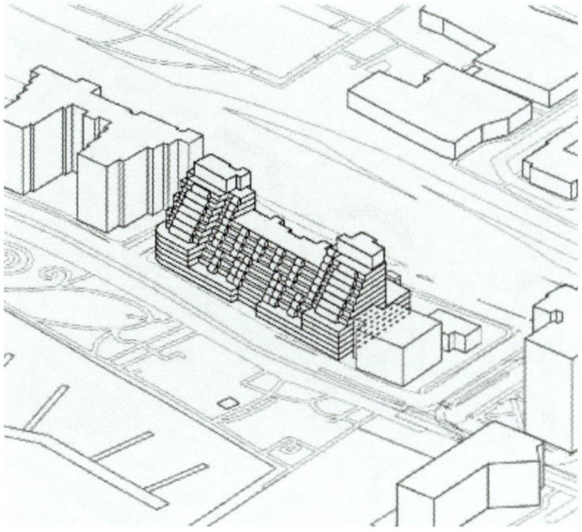

Travel in Canada

Understanding the challenges and opportunities facing the city of Edmonton and the proposed "Gateway Sites," the students embarked on an eight-day excursion into the urban and natural Canadian landscapes of Toronto, Edmonton, and Jasper National Park. At each location the students and the teaching team were joined by leaders and members of municipal, cultural, historical, design, and development organizations who lent their unique perspectives to the sites.

Day 1: Toronto
Housing Walking Tours

Portland Park Village

Hydro Block

Twenty Niagara Lofts

Ulster and Lippincott Streets laneway housing examples

Day 2: Toronto Housing Walking Tours

Breakfast conversation with architect and educator David Fortin on Metis Indigenous culture in Canada

Walking tour led by Joël León for Toronto Society of Architects

Tour and conversation on Regent Park Interpretation Strategy

Day 3: Toronto Tours and Discussion: Community Housing

Raymond Chow speaking on ongoing development at 2450 Victoria Park

Studio tours at 150 Dan Leckie Way

Day 4: Toronto
Tours and Discussion: Waterfront Toronto Offices

Conversations with Chris Glaisek, chief planning and design officer, before Toronto Waterfront walking tour

Students observe the unloading of a sugar shipment at Redpath Sugar Factory.

Day 5: Edmonton
Tour: Public Buildings and Legislative Grounds

The Maclab Theatre at the Citadel Theatre, in downtown Edmonton

Discussions on the origins of Borden Natural Swimming Pool with city officials

Day 6: Edmonton
Tours and Discussion: Maclab Development Group Holdings

Former Edmonton mayor Don Iveson was among the local professionals discussing the futures of their fields in Edmonton. Guests included Stephanie McCabe (City of Edmonton), Erik Backstrom (City of Edmonton), Susan McGee (Homeward Trust), Kim Sturgess (Alberta Water Smart), Bob Walker (Tangent Project Management), and Reese Rolheiser and Glen Fisher (ICI Canada).

Edmonton mayor Amarjeet Sohi meets with students, Claire Weisz, and Marc de La Bruyère (foreground).

Day 7: Jasper
Hiking and Exploration

Claire Weisz and studio members at Maligne Lake

Student Projects

Charis Armstrong
Maxwell Baum
Bingyu He
Zishi Li
Andrea Sanchez Moctezuma
Noah Sannes
Jahaan Scipio
Bishrelt Solongo
Brent Wafula
Jiaxing Yan

Students present final projects in Yale School of Architecture's Rudolph Hall.

Gold Bar Farm

Charis Armstrong
and Noah Sannes

Edmonton is a rapidly expanding city. Its current government has elected to resist urban sprawl and encourage densification through novel urban policies. However these policies risk inflating the cost of housing. Within neighborhoods like Gold Bar, an aging population and housing stock pose a challenge for the transition from an isolated suburban environment to an enriched intergenerational care community.

This project, located on the former site of Gold Bar Farm, seeks to introduce contemporary elderly housing that embraces living solutions at scales new to Edmonton and for less-served populations such as elders within the LGBTQ+ community. Laneway Accessory Dwelling Units (ADUs) and adjacent town homes provide transitional down-sized housing for elders and extended family members. Those requiring more assistance have various care options within tightly knit "ravine apartment" enclaves. Defined by diverse residential offerings, carefully renovated historic buildings, and outdoor amenities that connect the site with an expansive ravine trail network, the development encourages a strengthened relationship between the natural environment and generations of Edmontonians.

Gold Bar Farm

Charis Armstrong and Noah Sannes

Aerial view of Gold Bar Farm proposal from southeast

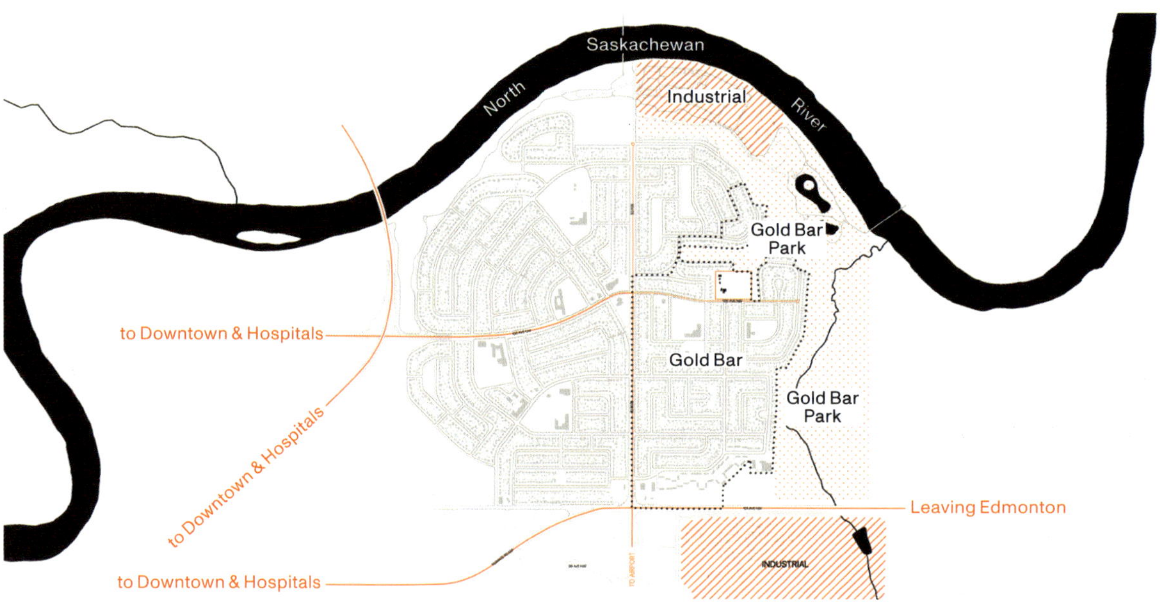

Gold Bar Farm location, transit connectivity to Edmonton, and position in relation to industrial and natural areas

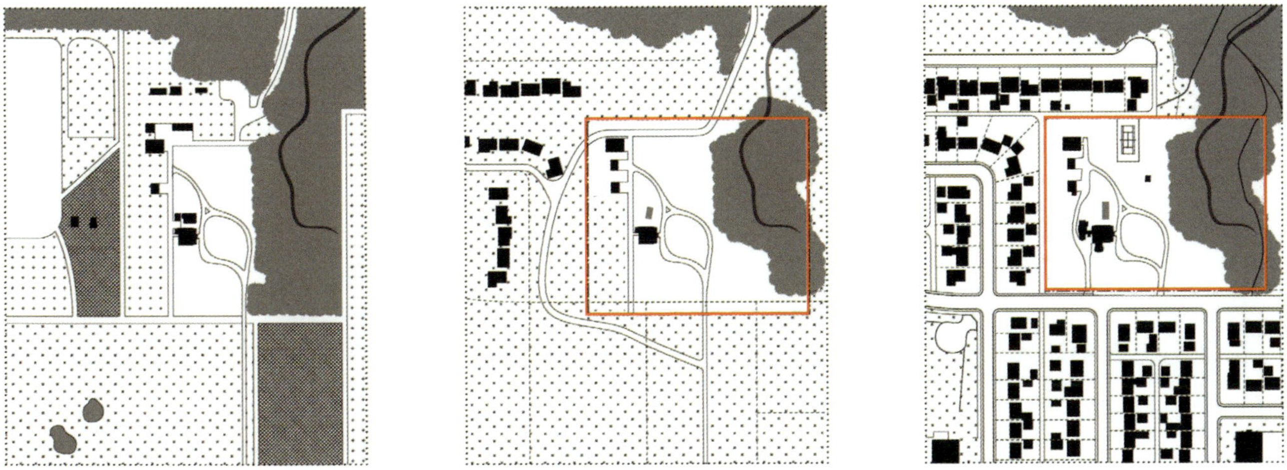

Gold Bar Farm site during its early years as a working farm in 1948, at the beginning of single-family home construction in 1957, and in 2022

Aerial photograph of Gold Bar Farm, circa 1940

Gold Bar Farm in 2022

Gold Bar Farm

Charis Armstrong and Noah Sannes

Opportunities between Laneway ADU homes for parking structures to serve as community gathering points

Gold Bar Farm

Charis Armstrong
and Noah Sannes

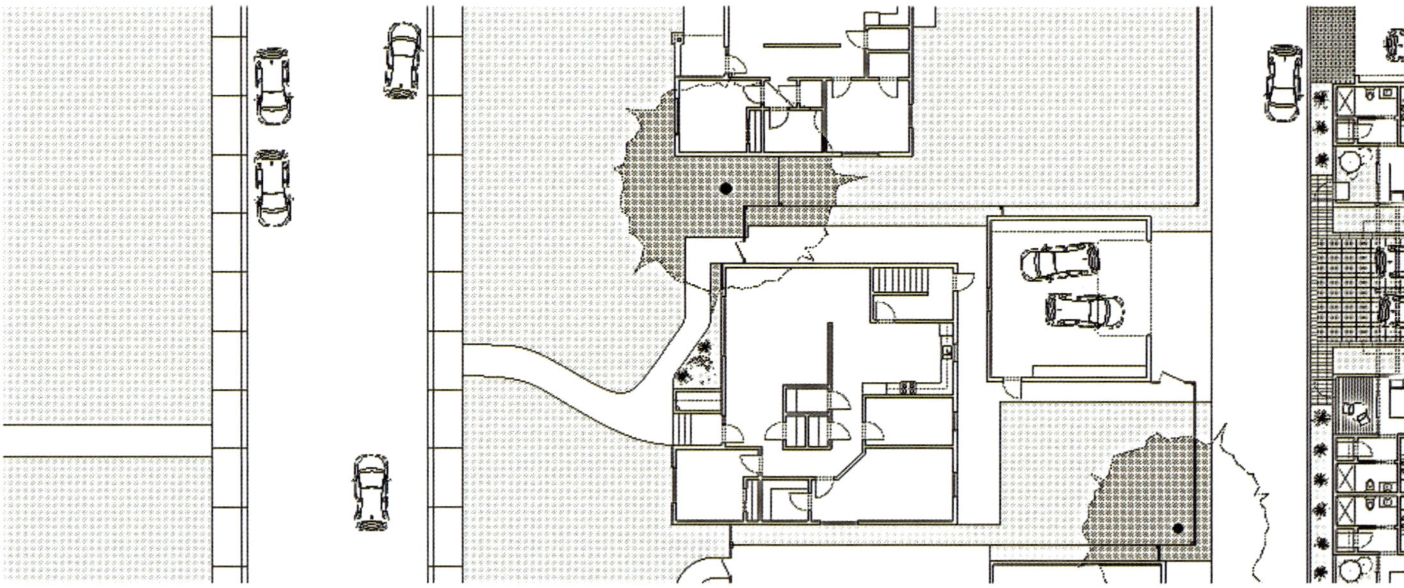

First-floor plan of existing single-family housing typologies, Laneway ADU home, Townhome, and assisted-living Ravine Apartment structures

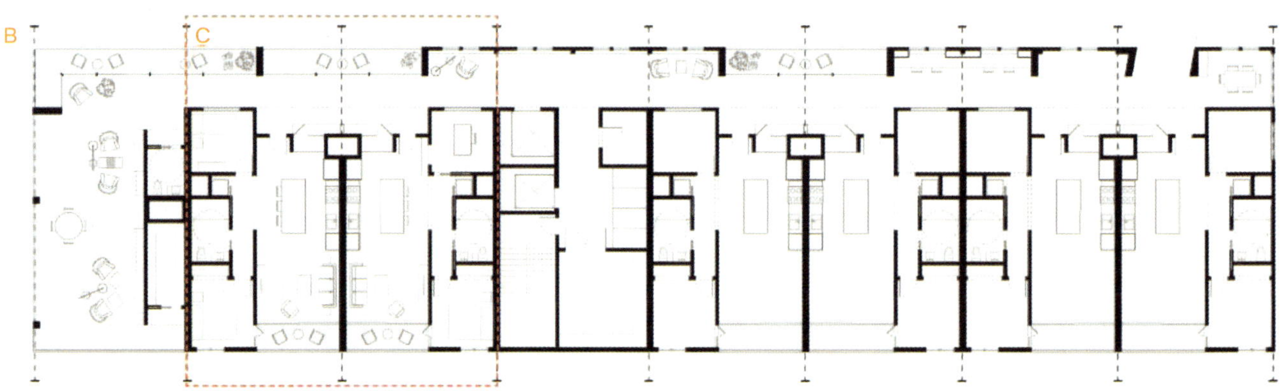

Sample apartment floor plan showing community spaces, activated hallway porches, and unit layouts

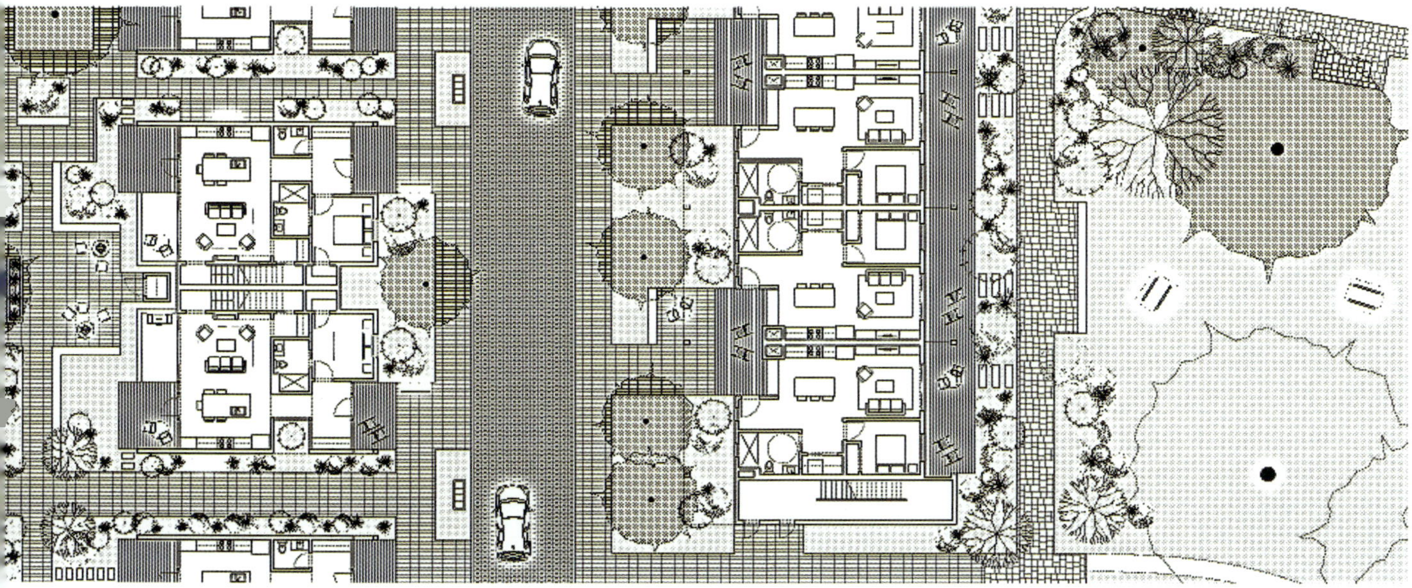

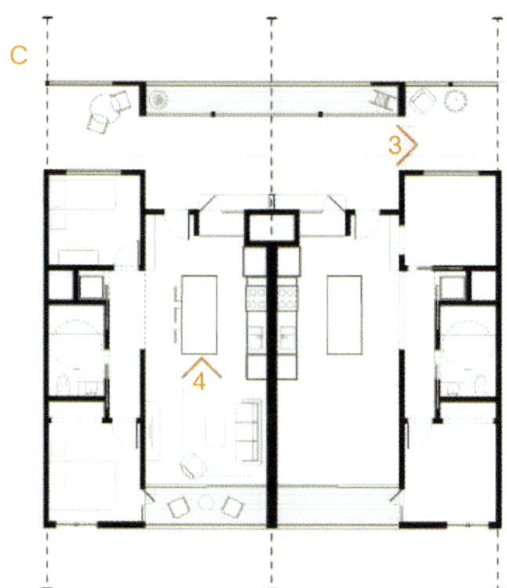

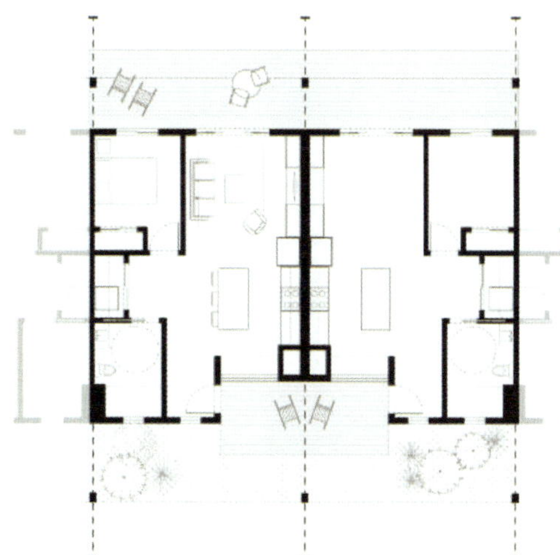

Upper-floor and ground-floor typical unit arrangements, view of activated internal porches (3), and interior living spaces (4)

Apartment single-loaded corridors provide an internal street with personalized "porches"

Student Projects

Gold Bar Farm

Charis Armstrong and Noah Sannes

Site Area

6.5 Acres

Residential Unit Count

117

Estimated Land Value

$8,000,000

Hard Construction Costs

$41,250,000

Soft Construction Costs

$7,500,000

Rent Range

$1,250–$3,500

Residential Annual Gross Potential Revenue

$216,563

Pro Forma Data

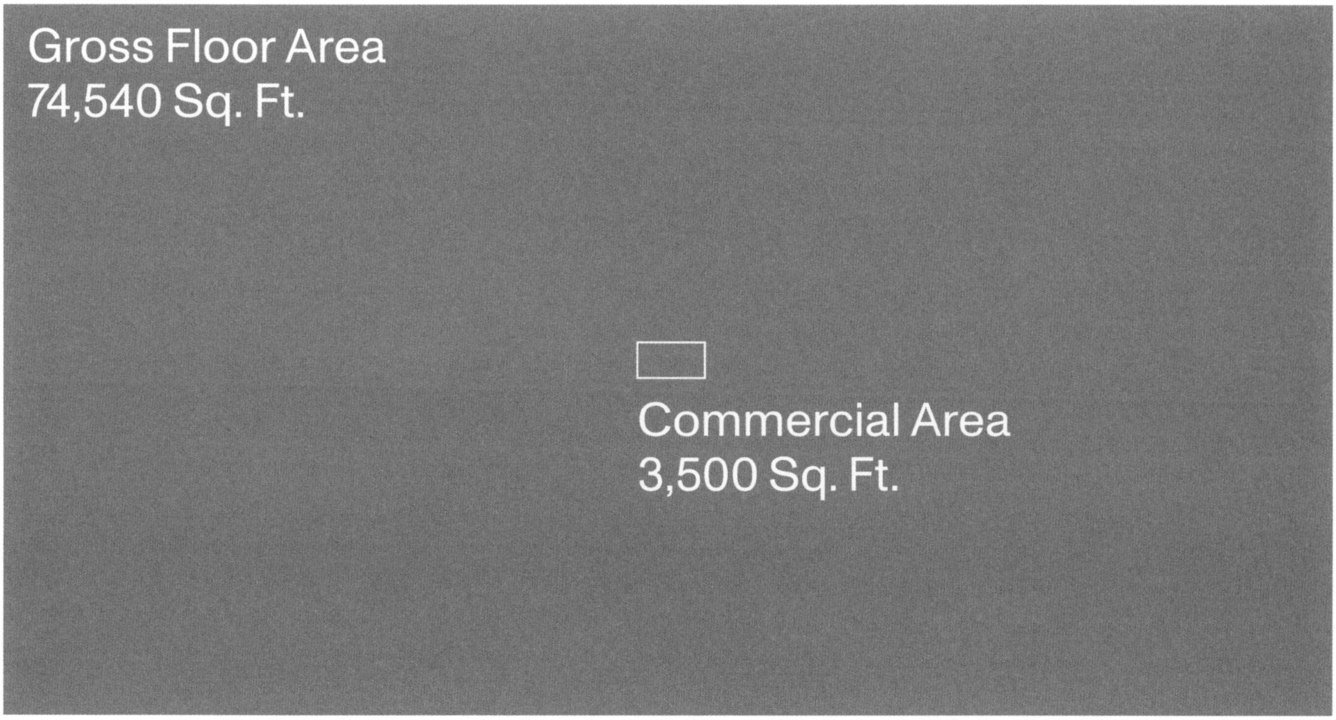

Non-residential Programming

Community Spaces,
Private Event Spaces, Cafe,
Barbershop / Salon,
After-school Center,
Community Health Center,
Transport Assistance Center,
Parking

Commercial Annual Gross Potential Revenue

$305,556

Total Net Operating Income

$2,681,250

Most Likely: A Case for the Better

Andrea Sanchez Moctezuma
and Jahaan Scipio

Located in a ravine off the North Saskatchewan River, this project roots itself in the notion of "reciprocal development" and the provocation that a development may pursue increased commercial and residential density alongside the "development" of the land and its natural, communal resources. In a dual process of construction and afforestation, the project utilizes recreational ravine land to densify a suburban enclave by establishing a partnership with the city that trades development rights for improved park infrastructure. Considering the development over a lifespan of fifty years, the work also seeks to understand the natural and anthropogenic conditions of the last 15,000 years, paying attention to the ways we manipulate nature to reflect cultural attitudes, norms, and needs. Learning from the laneway to produce a formal language that is incremental, nuanced, and ripe with activity, "Most Likely" approaches the unavoidable issue of densification with a focus on the productivity of exchange.

The ravine-growth project explores new strategies for building a sustainable community that can exist in the context of an economy where affordability is not subsidized primarily by the public. Our illustrative chronologies explore the transitional growth of the ravine as it is allowed to continue its path through the community. The idea of the project is to allow nature to follow its organic trajectory, instead of domesticating the borders and delimitations of the forest, and the dwelling community to grow, shift, and develop around nature instead of the other way around. Edmonton's northern isolation and its ability to supply workforce housing with minimal government subsidy sets up a laboratory for solving emerging societal challenges. Here there is an opportunity to explore new models of development in the Anthropocene era in which sustainability, resiliency, and cultural cognizance align design and development interests.

Most Likely: A Case for the Better

Andrea Sanchez Moctezuma and Jahaan Scipio

Forest land is interwoven with structures that serve to elevate housing to reduce impact on lower-story growth over time and negotiate the intense grade changes across the ravine-edge site.

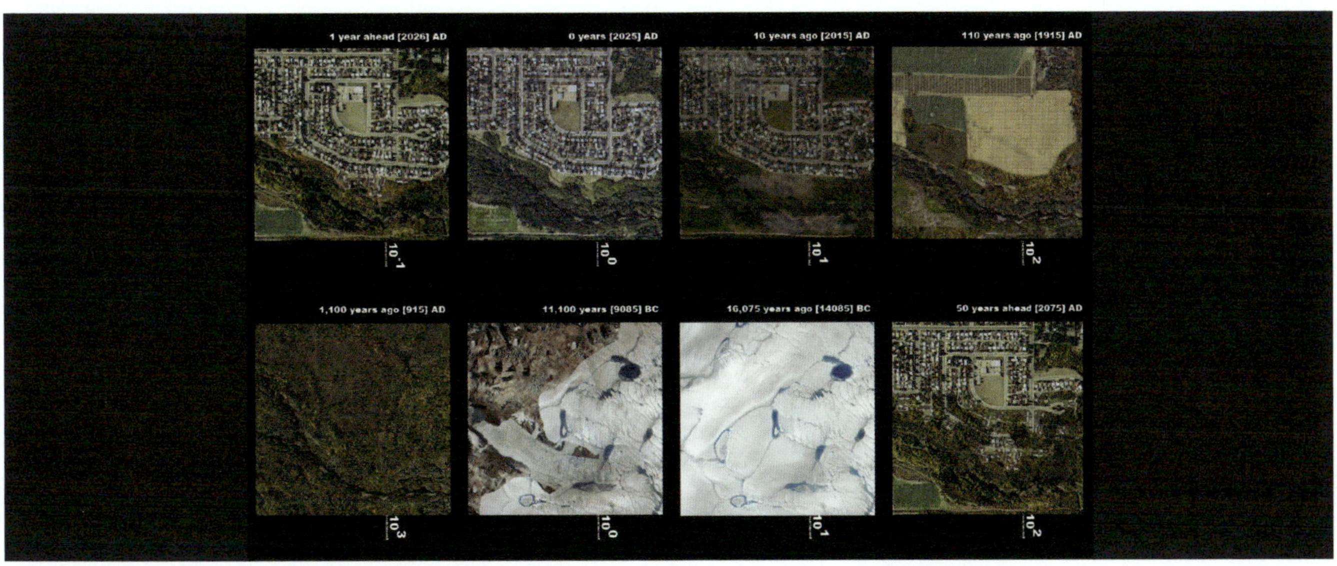

Drawing inspiration from the Eames Office's film Powers of Ten, the site is contextualized in relation to its agricultural history in the recent past, its anthropogenic development over the last 15,000 years, and a possible future ravine development adjacent to Gold Bar Park at varying scales.

Most Likely: A Case for the Better

Andrea Sanchez Moctezuma and Jahaan Scipio

Possible floor-plan configuration of the ravine housing block

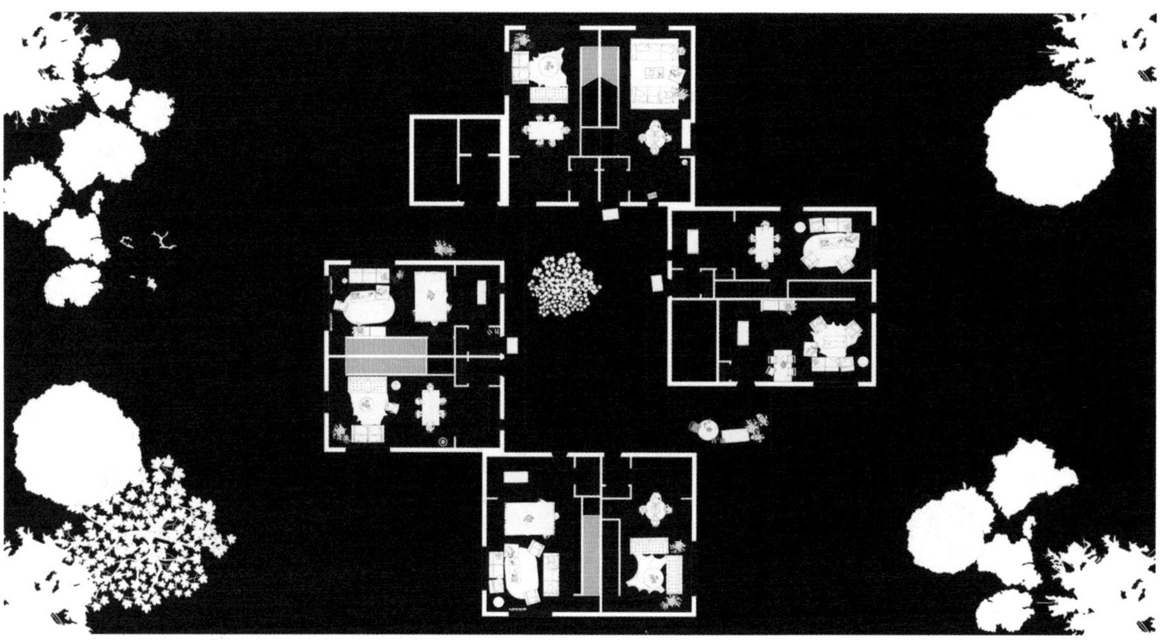

Secondary floor-plan configuration providing an enclosed courtyard at ground level

The structures' elevated floor plans position the homes in the upper story of the forest and provide views into the parkland.

Most Likely: A Case for the Better

Andrea Sanchez Moctezuma and Jahaan Scipio

Elevation of the laneway as transformed through the residential development, lower forest growth, and community activations of food vendors and local programs

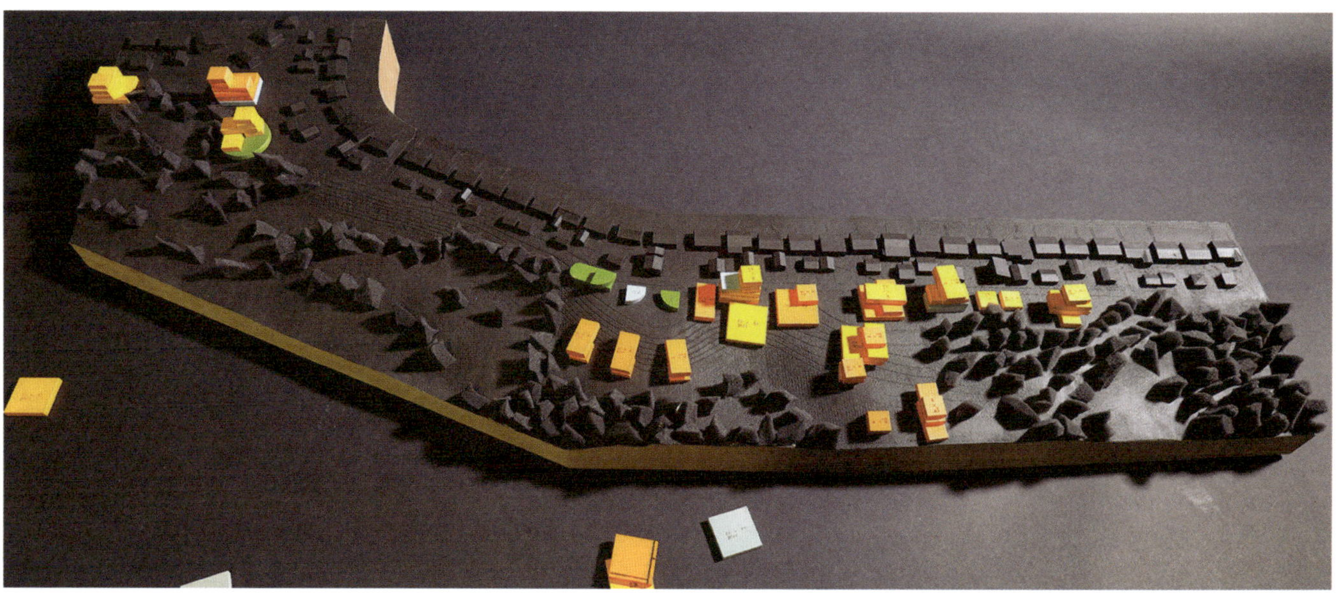

Early planning tools for visualizing the physical impact of certain programmatic interventions on the site

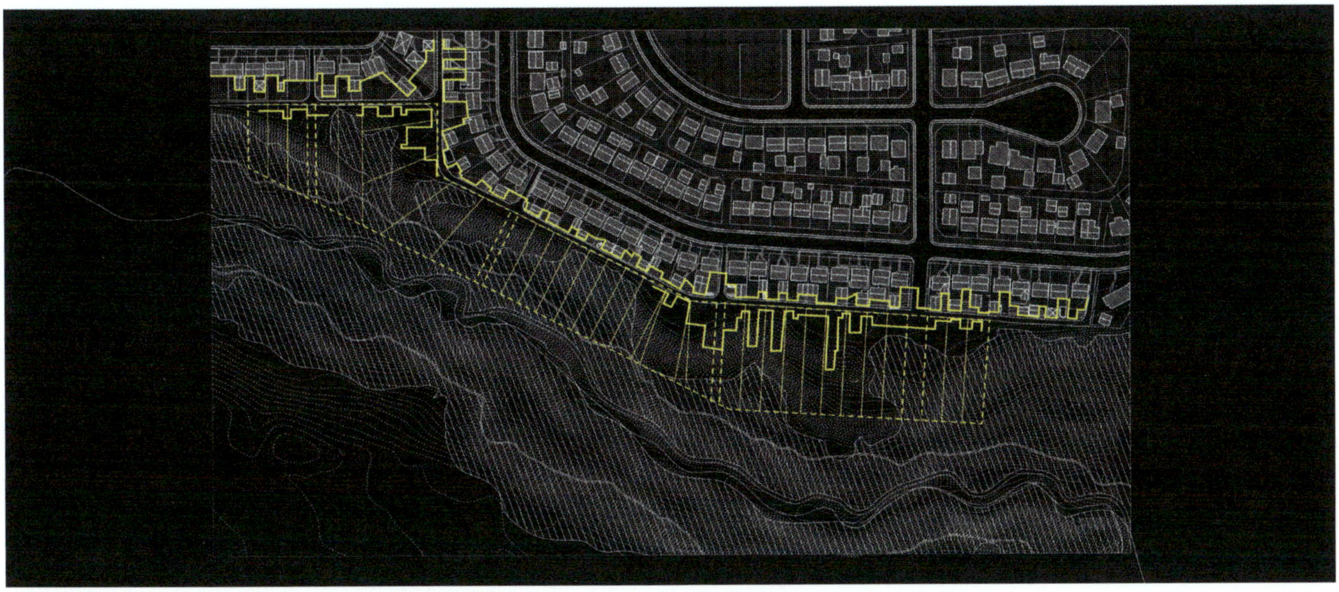

Drawing from laneway housing precedents in Toronto, the proposed project parcels suggest a staggered relationship with the laneway that negotiates space between new development and neighbors to the north

Most Likely: A Case for the Better

Andrea Sanchez Moctezuma and Jahaan Scipio

Site Area

9.71 Acres

Residential Unit Count

78

Hard Construction Costs

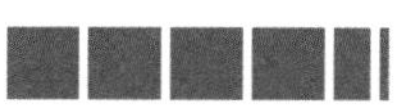

$41,250,000

Rent Range

$1,800

Soft Construction Costs

$9,938,467

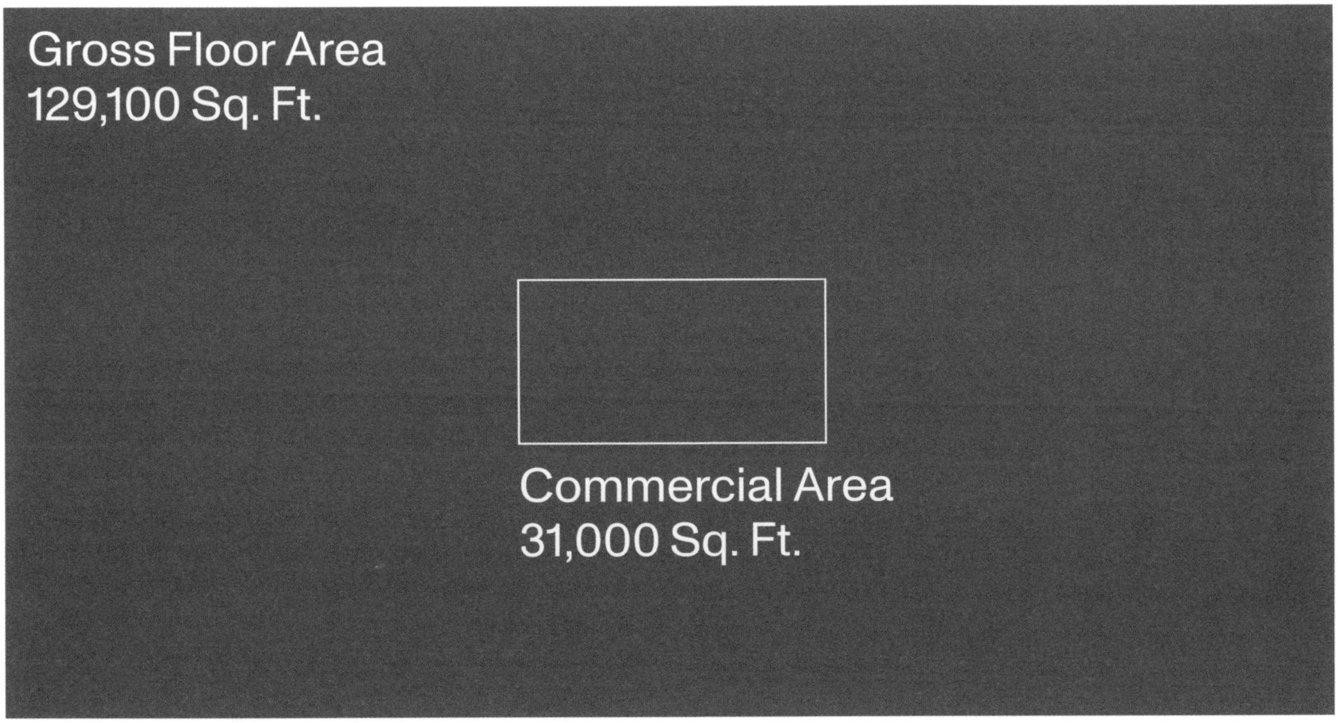

Non-residential Programming

"Mom-and-Pop" Shop, Retail, Cafes, Event Space, Equipment Rental, Gyms, Community Greenhouses/ Public Spaces, Parking Garage

Commercial Annual Gross Potential Revenue

$1,348,836

Total Net Operating Income

$2,433,836

The Farmers, The Artists, Their Homes, and Their Spa

Zishi Li
and Jiaxing Yan

Inspired by Edmonton's call for energy transition strategies, we would collaborate with local vertical farming businesses to propose a development project consisting of two properties in order to revamp the status quo on Edmonton's east border, which is both industry-heavy and arbitrarily defined. Following the logic of urban food production concerning farming, distribution, retail, embodied carbon, and waste management, we speculate how spatial assets may be continuously adapted and reused by various groups in newly densified neighborhoods.

With two parcels totaling 19.5 acres that are 850 feet apart (a three-minute walk), the two featured properties are industrial and residential, curbing the city's shortage of durable industrial buildings and multifamily housing. Through this combination, we seek not only to activate the interstitial area between the Gold Bar Neighborhood and Eastgate Business Park but also to push for an expansion of the current public transit system with a new LRT station stop on-site. Community greenhouses along the highway block off noise and pollution as shared public space between Rivervalley Townhomes and the new housing. The unique sloping ETFE pillow facade of the residential program provides ample insulation for cold months on two levels of atria.

The Farmers, The Artists, Their Homes, and Their Spa

Zishi Li and Jiaxing Yan

Residential parcel and industrial parcel urban relationships

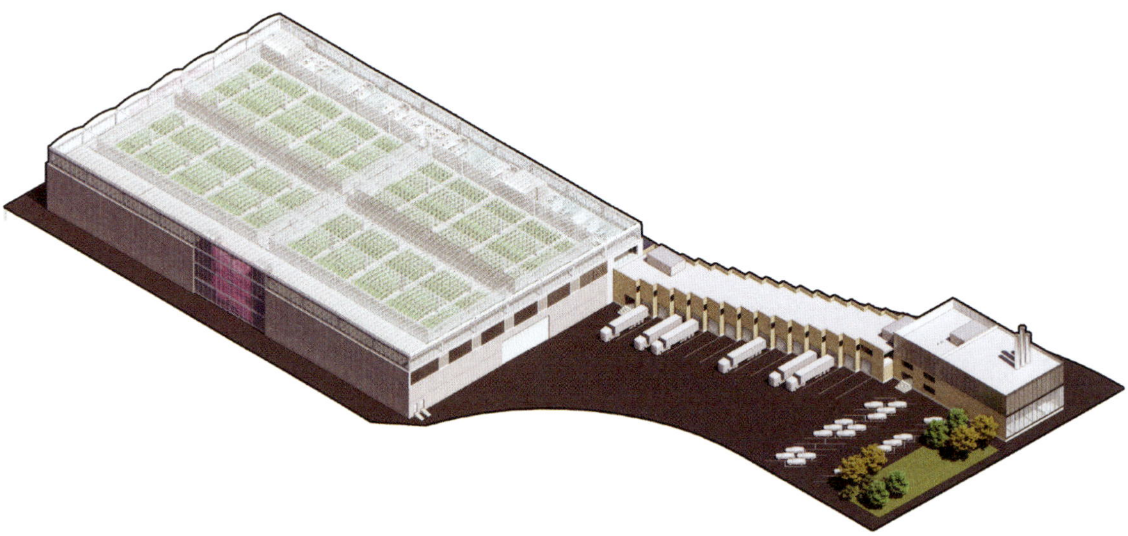

Phase 1 of industrial parcel, vertical farming only

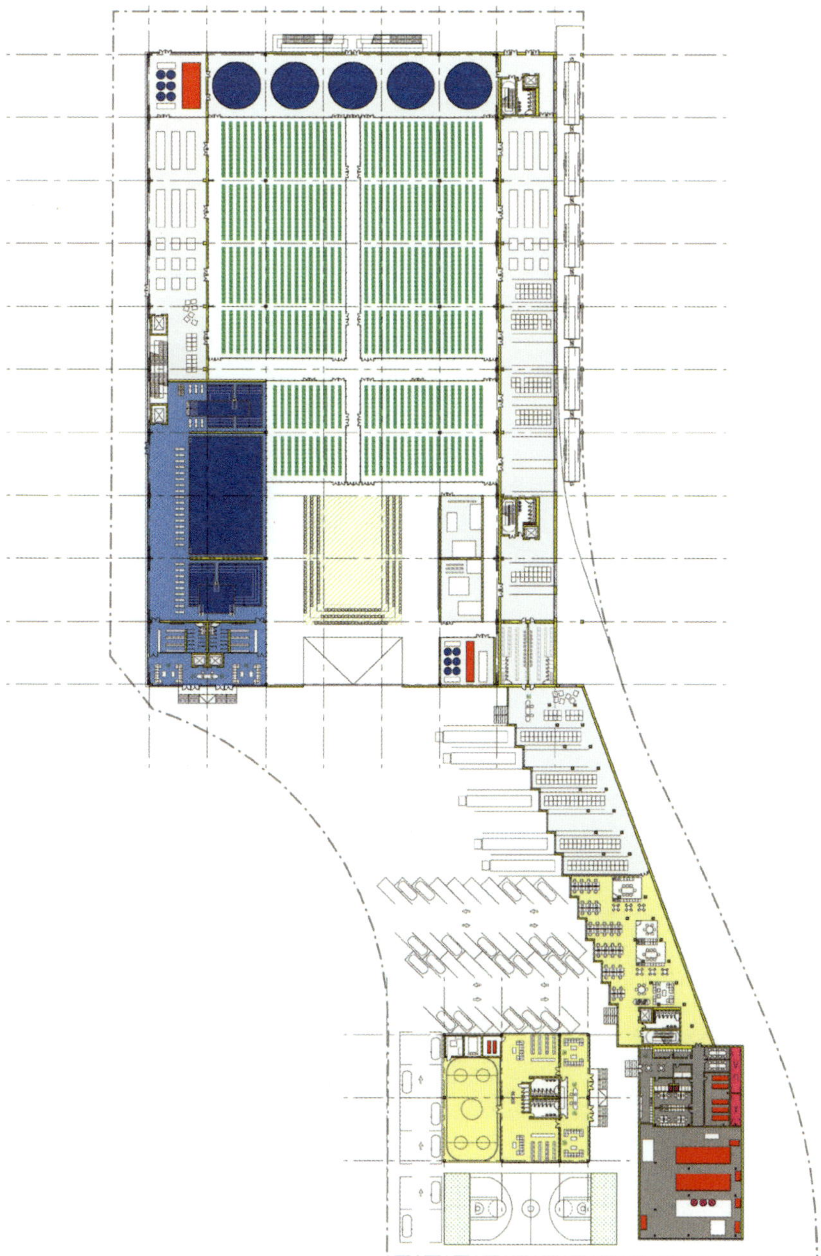

Phase 3, Level 1: Ground-floor shipping/receiving, growing, water storage, management offices, and public performance spaces

The Farmers, The Artists, Their Homes, and Their Spa

Zishi Li and Jiaxing Yan

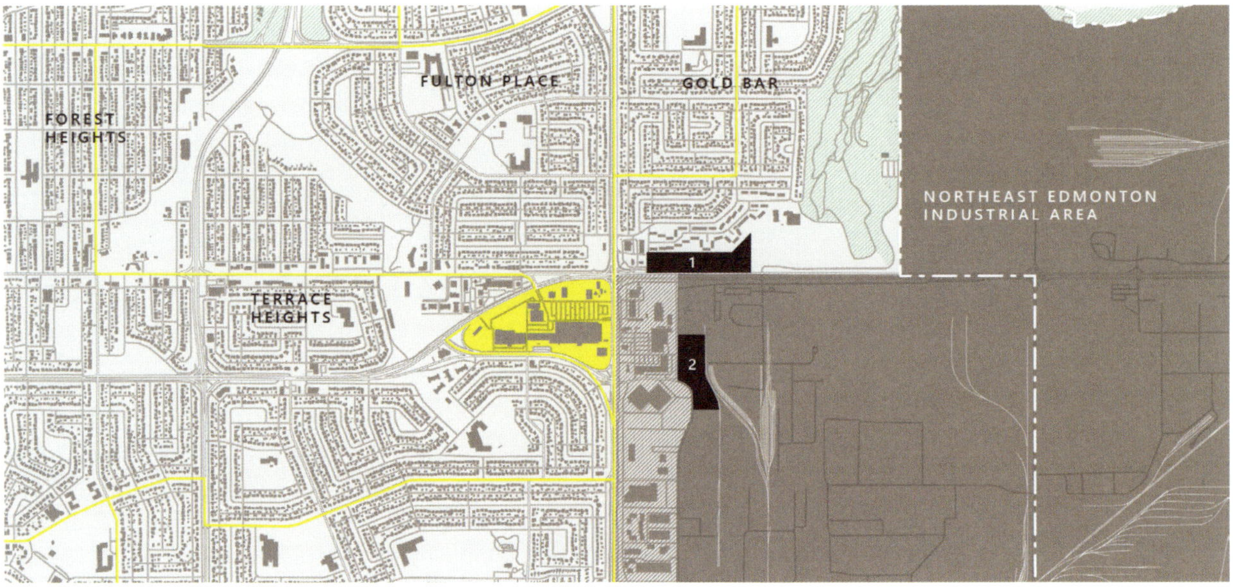

Residential parcel (1) and industrial parcel (2) gateway relationship to suburban and industrial zones, 3 phases over 10 years until completion

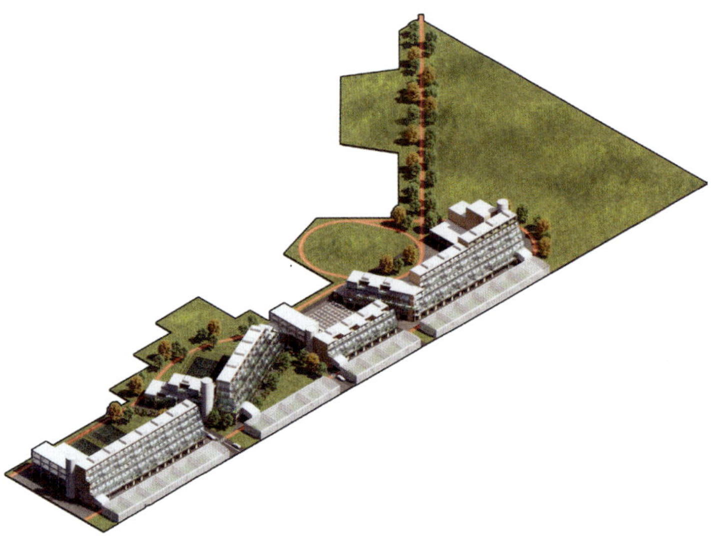

Relation of running track extending to ravine with residential buildings, ground-floor retail, and community greenhouses

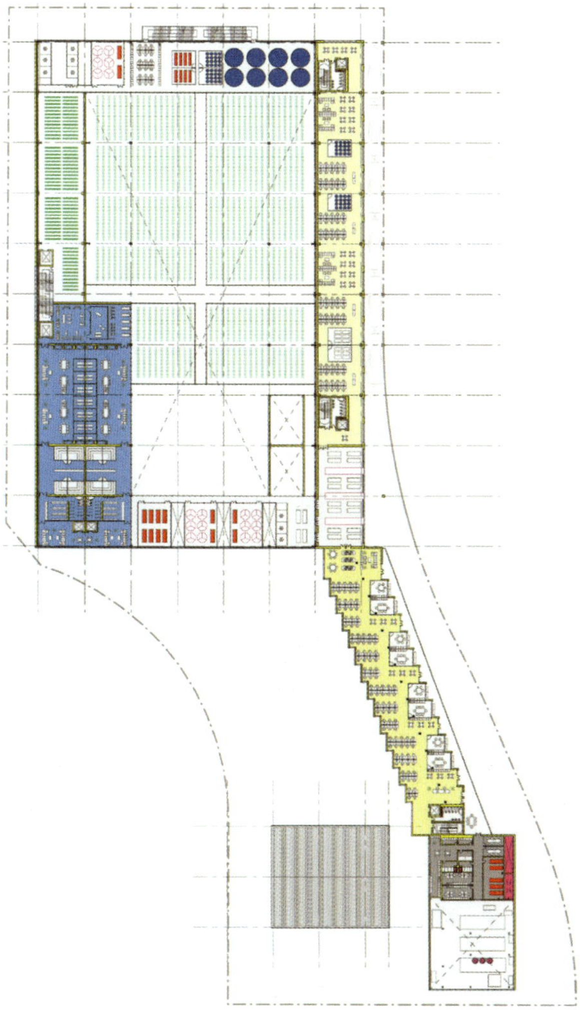

Phase 3, Level 2: Mechanical floor, artist and community work, and performance spaces

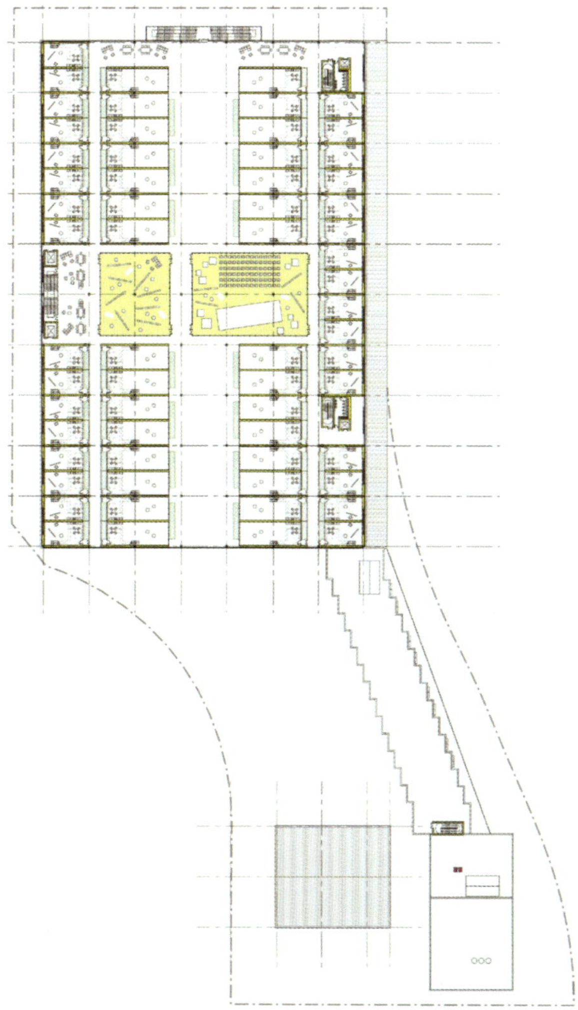

Phase 3, Level 3: Greenhouse floor removed with artist residences and community performance space filling former growing space

The Farmers, The Artists, Their Homes, and Their Spa

Zishi Li and Jiaxing Yan

Sloping ETFE pillow facade at residential levels as viewed from the northeast

The Farmers, The Artists, Their Homes, and Their Spa

Zishi Li
and Jiaxing Yan

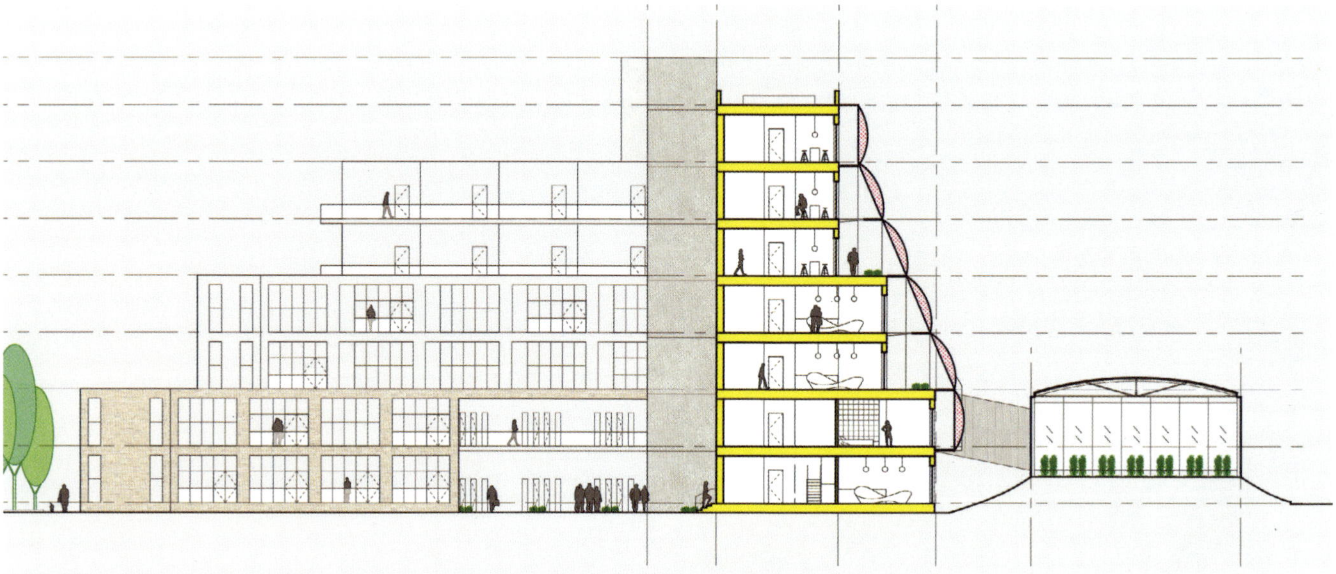

Residential parcel (1) and industrial parcel (2) gateway relationship to suburban and industrial zones, 3 phases over 10 years until completion

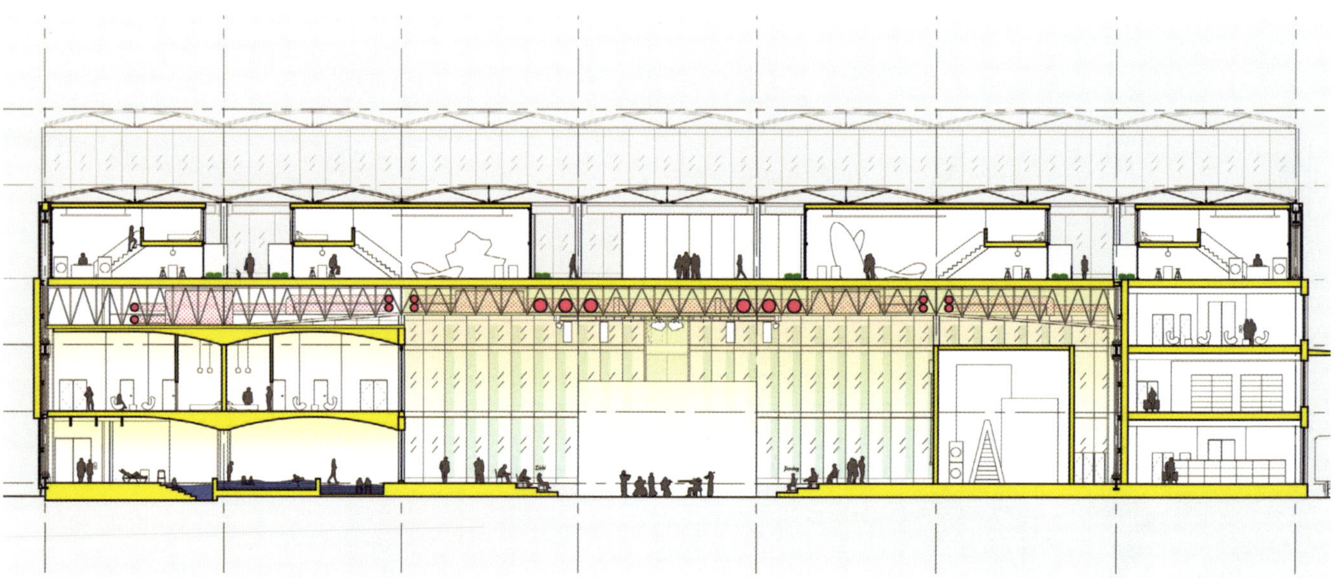

Phase 1 of industrial parcel, vertical farming only

Student Projects

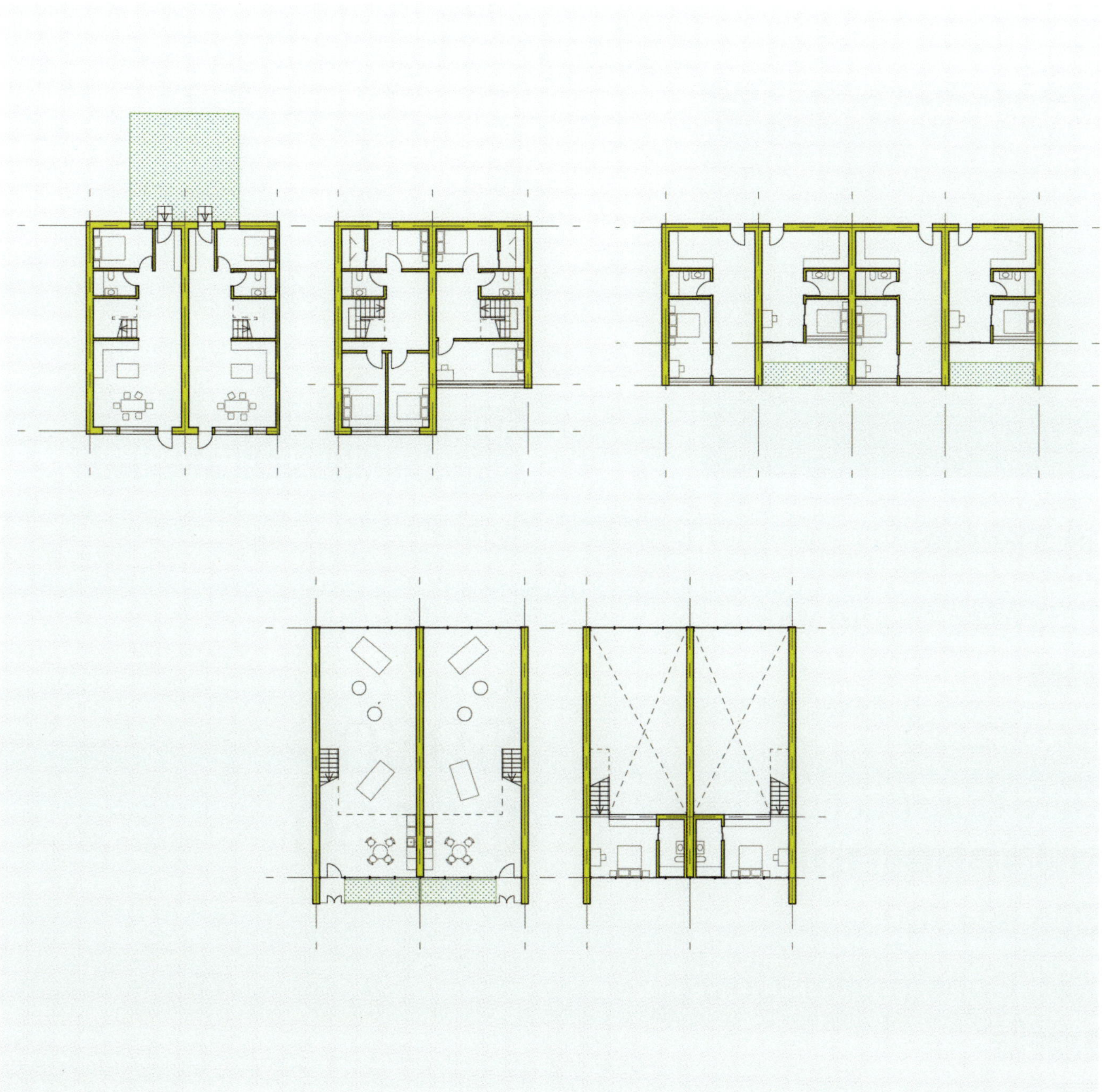

Typical unit plan types

The Farmers, The Artists, Their Homes, and Their Spa

Zishi Li and Jiaxing Yan

Site Area

19.5 Acres

Estimated Land Value

$4,062,520

Hard Construction Costs*

$65,394,700

Soft Construction Costs*

$5,930,000

Residential Unit Count

321

Rent Range

$960–$1,560

*data for Industrial Parcel only

Gross Floor Area
297,186 Sq. Ft.

Non-residential Programming

Vertical Farming, Distribution Center, Exhibition Space, Employment Center, Skating Pavilion, Spa, Pool, Flex Theatre, Parking, Power Plant

Commercial Annual Gross Potential Revenue*

$8,566,480

Total Net Operating Income*

$6,835,968

Empire Park

Bingyu He
and Maxwell Baum

This project contends with the reality of property development and architecture. In a city of many transient workers, immigrant families, and short-term young professionals, there is a challenge to provide adequate flexible and affordable housing.

The goal of this master plan is to facilitate the conditions of "community" and "collective" through a focus on program, infrastructure, and landscape and to foster a site of arrival for transient people and immigrants, among others. The site is oriented to create a sense of "permeable interiority" where a dense multifamily, mixed-use housing "frame" supports a landscape focused education and community-oriented interior.

This strategy draws upon the existing Edmontonian typology of the "community league," where a large public park area is paired and co-situated with a public school system.

Redeveloping and densifying the underused site of Empire Park will provide an accessible active space for the increasing demand Edmonton is facing while creating an environment that can provide support for families, renters, and existing adjacent residents.

The superimposition of program and living and the mixed-use, dense nature of the urban fabric provides opportunities for bolstering community and the interaction of residents. This site of pedestrian and multimodal vehicular mobility can attain an identity of destination instead of being simply a place for commuting. The overall composition of the program would integrate into the larger framework of the area by focusing on access to bus lines, the mall, and the adjacent neighborhoods to provide a walkable public-transit-focused residential area to live in for both short and extended periods.

Empire Park

Bingyu He and Maxwell Baum

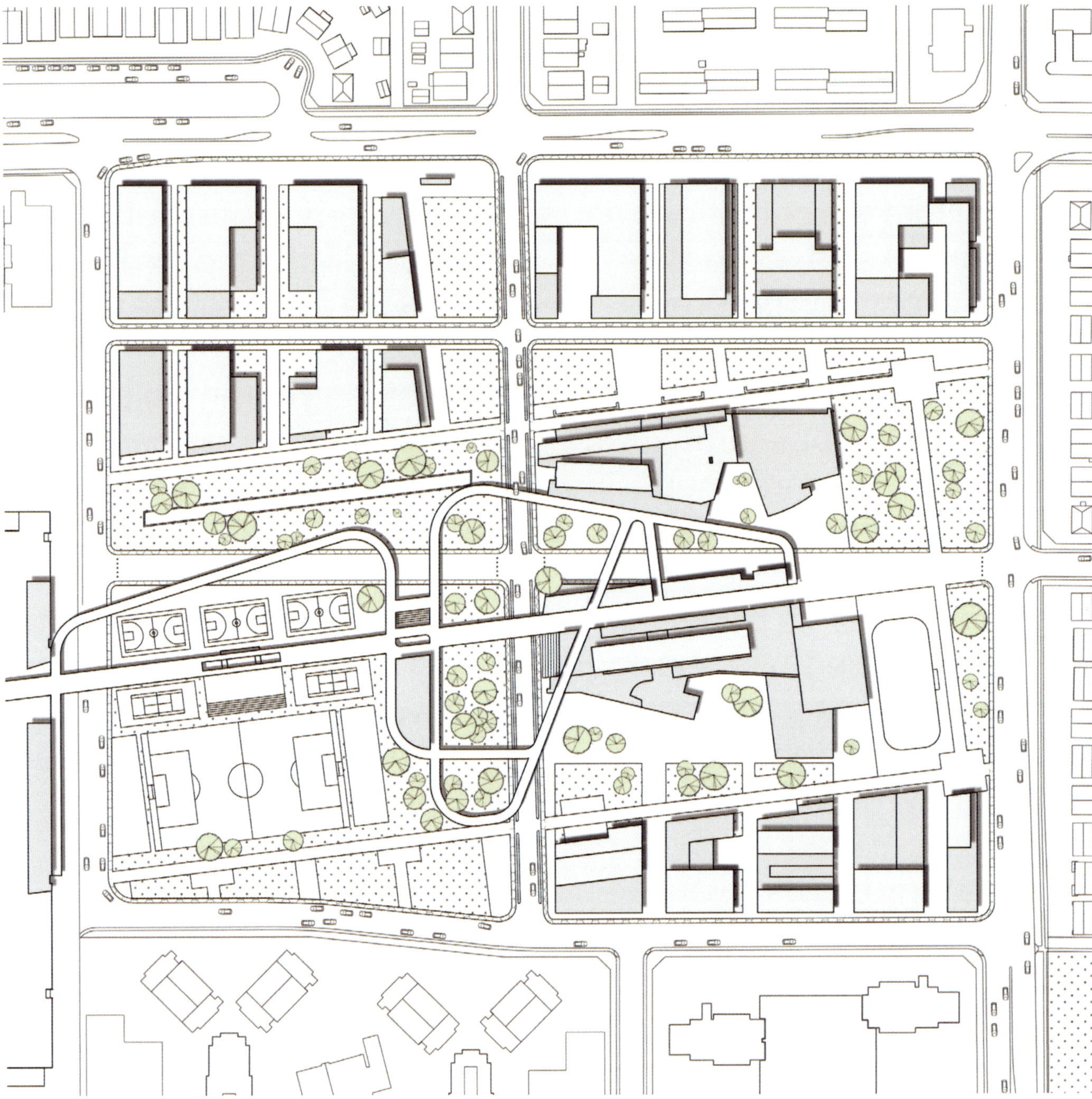

Development proposal master plan

Student Projects

Internal pavement and roadways are limited in quantity and direction, sharing paved space with bicycle lanes.

Empire Park

Bingyu He
and Maxwell Baum

Perspective along limited roadways in the development

Empire Park

Bingyu He
and Maxwell Baum

Sectional relationship of the Empire Park proposal

Empire Park

Bingyu He
and Maxwell Baum

Laneway-like parkways between residential blocks become a unique community space.

04

Pedestrians are prioritized within elevated walkways, allowing them to negotiate Edmonton's snowy winter conditions.

Empire Park

Bingyu He
and Maxwell Baum

Aerial perspective of the proposal with Southgate Centre and Village at Southgate in the foreground

Student Projects

Empire Park

Bingyu He
and Maxwell Baum

Site Area

21.93 Acres

Residential Unit Count

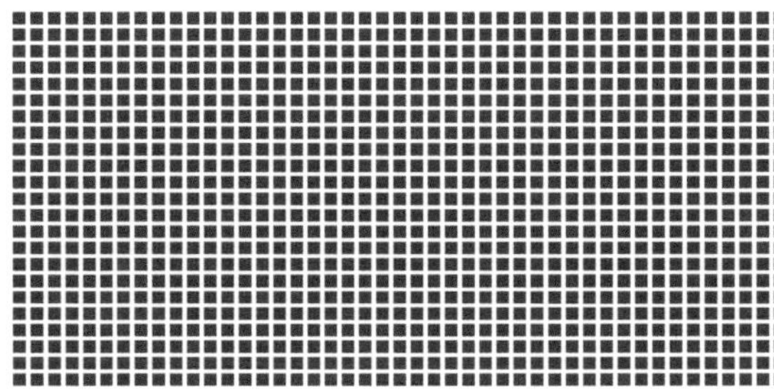

1080

Gross Floor Area
1,300,000 Sq. Ft.

Non-residential Programming

Workshops (Art), Gallery, Work Space, Parks, Childcare Bike Storage & Maintenance, Library, Flexible Classrooms, Meeting Space, Maker-Space, Greenhouses, Indigenous Culture Center

A Case for the Better

Bishrelt Solongo
and Brent Wafula

Our project was focused on harnessing the capacity of architecture to encourage healthy routine and movement with the deployment of development tools. Responding to the twenty first century imperative for sustainable lifestyles, the Pleasantview Townhomes Gateway Site was chosen for a pedestrian-centered proposal steps away from the local retail Southgate Center.

The site provides an excellent opportunity to integrate various renewable methods due to the low density of its proposed housing stock. Adjacent lots were also examined for the implementation of renewable-energy production methods, such as geothermal, solar energy, and wind power. The proximity of the Southgate center and park zone offered ideal conditions for accessing sustainable resources. Repurposing stormwater in the form of a central water body, for example, allowed for the creation of a pond within the project that facilitated thermal mitigation to the benefit of the surrounding building systems. In an effort to create reciprocal relationships between neighborhoods and municipalities, surplus solar energy collected across the site would contribute to the city power grid.

A Case for the Better

Bishrelt Solongo
and Brent Wafula

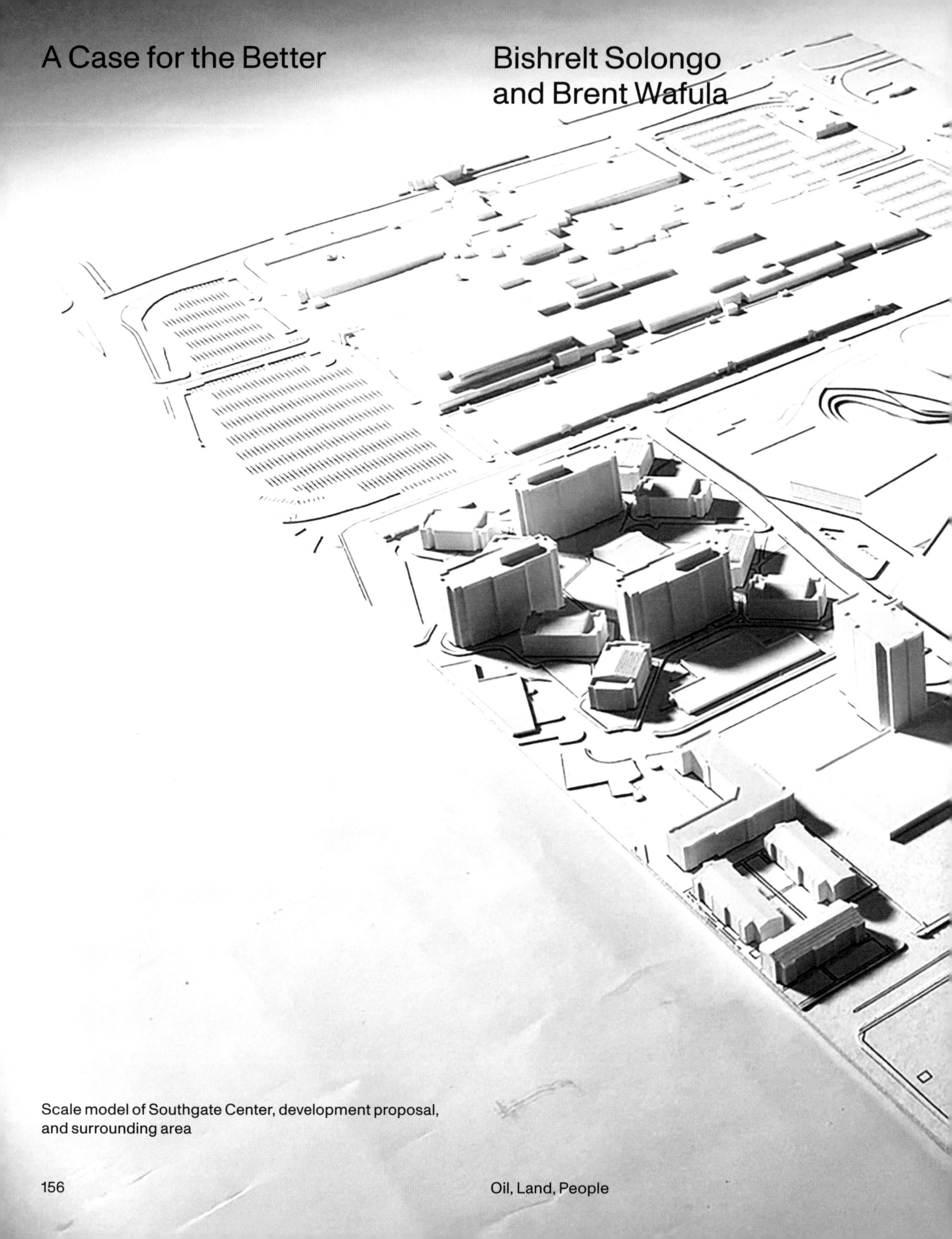

Scale model of Southgate Center, development proposal, and surrounding area

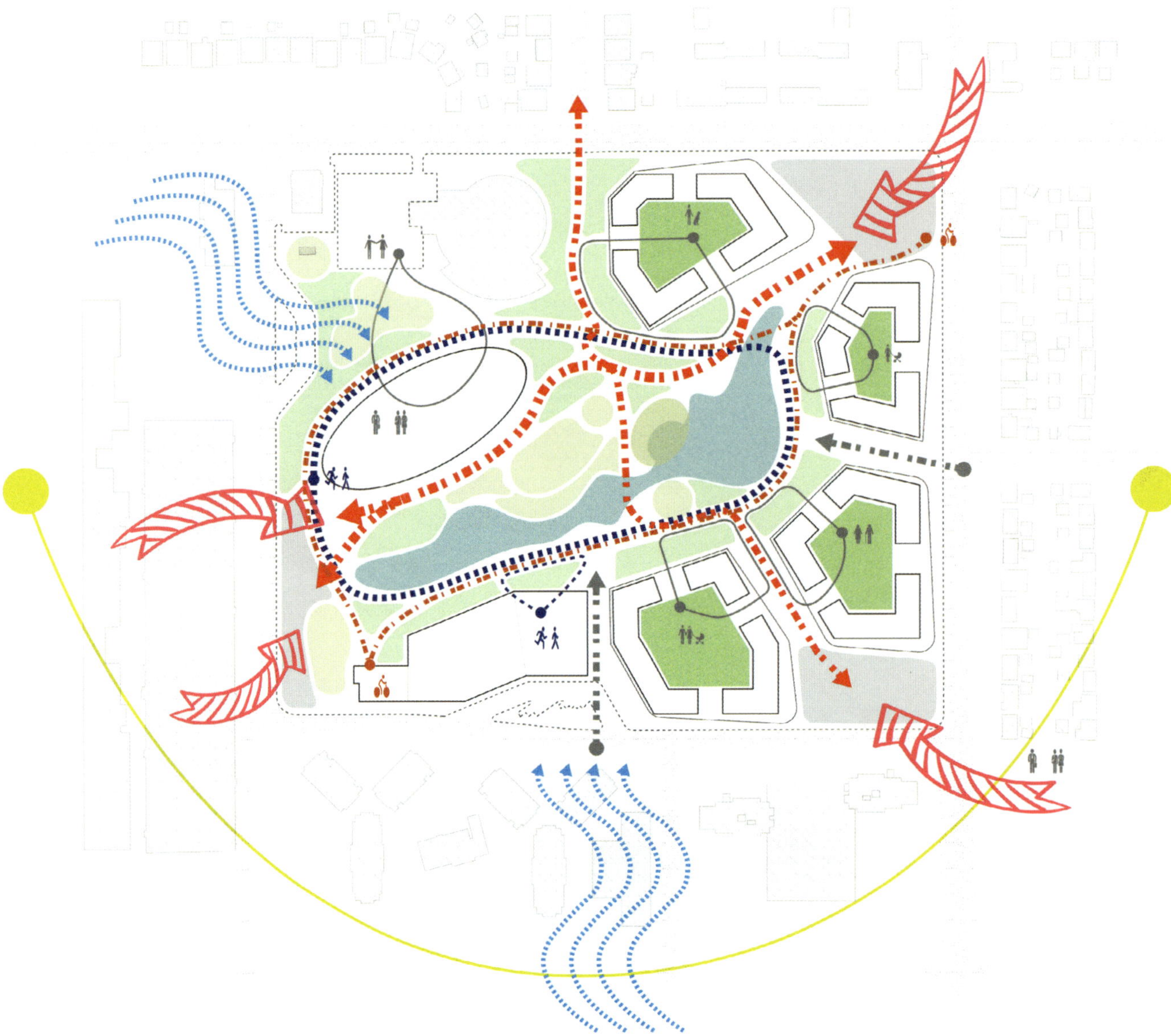

Diagram of site strategy and natural conditions

Student Projects

Site program master plan and planting vision

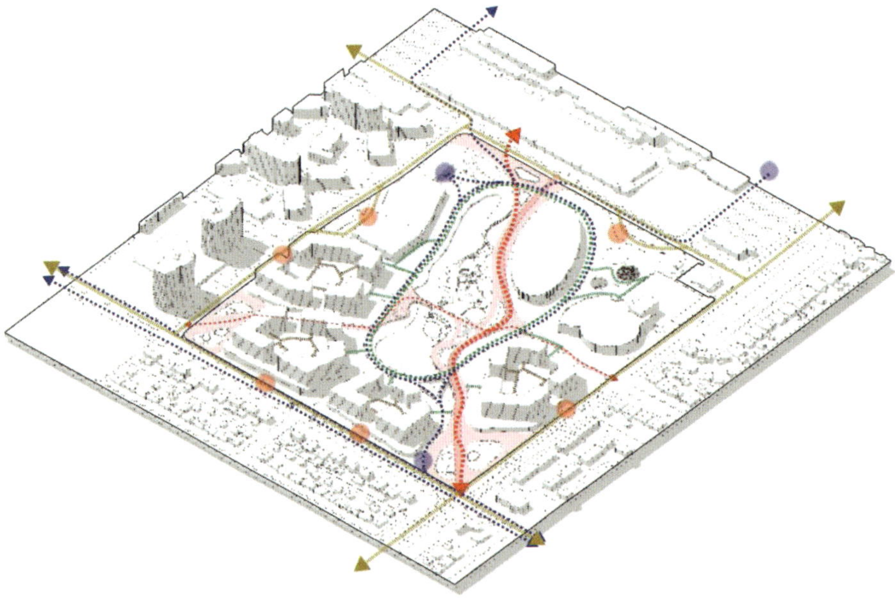

Circulation diagram

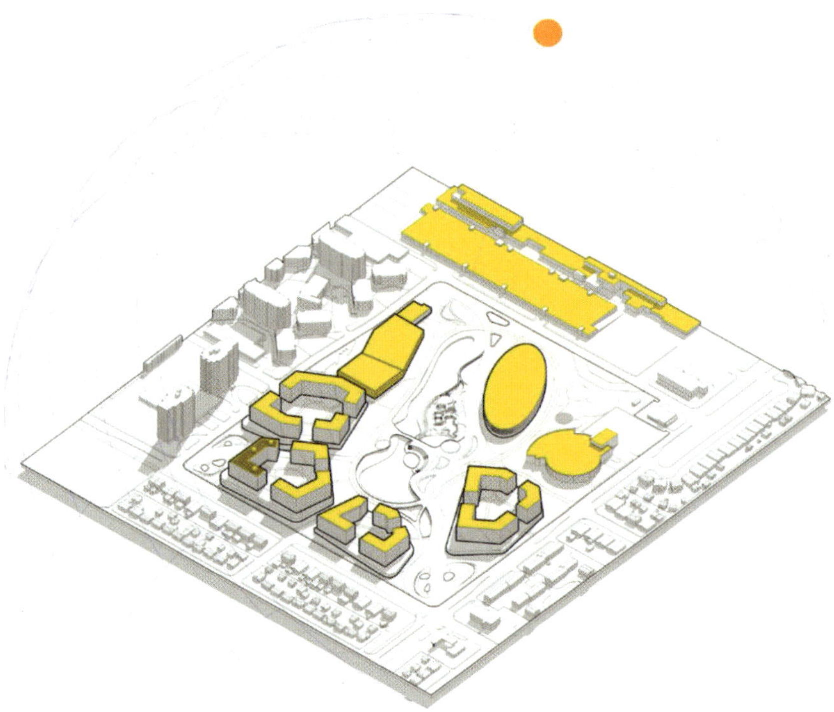

Development solar strategies

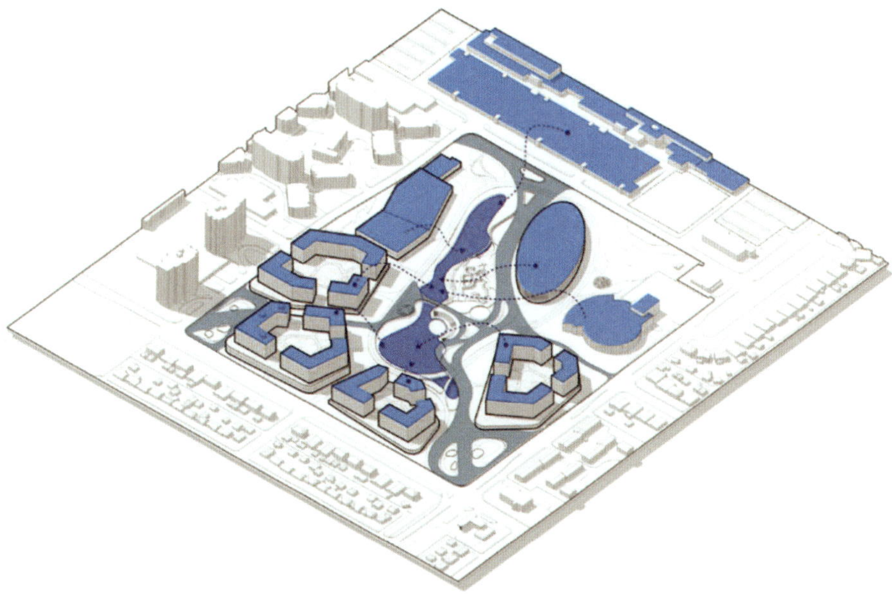

Development water-management plan and precipitation study

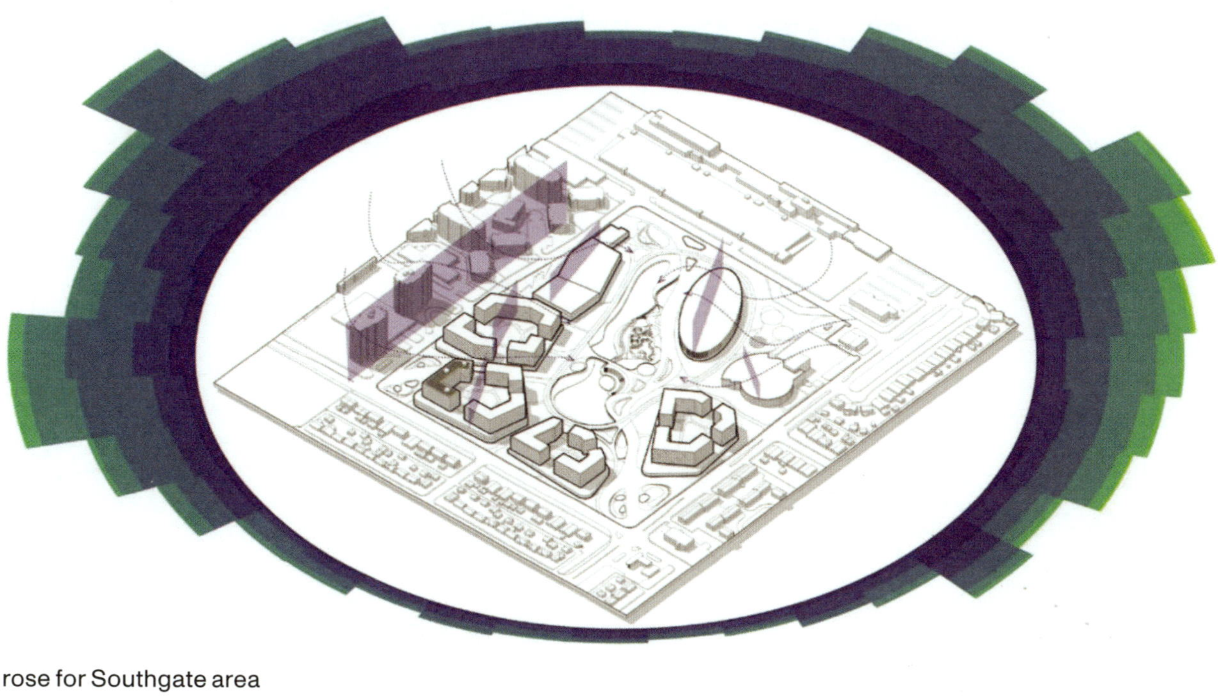

Wind rose for Southgate area

Edmonton timeline and inspirations for future development

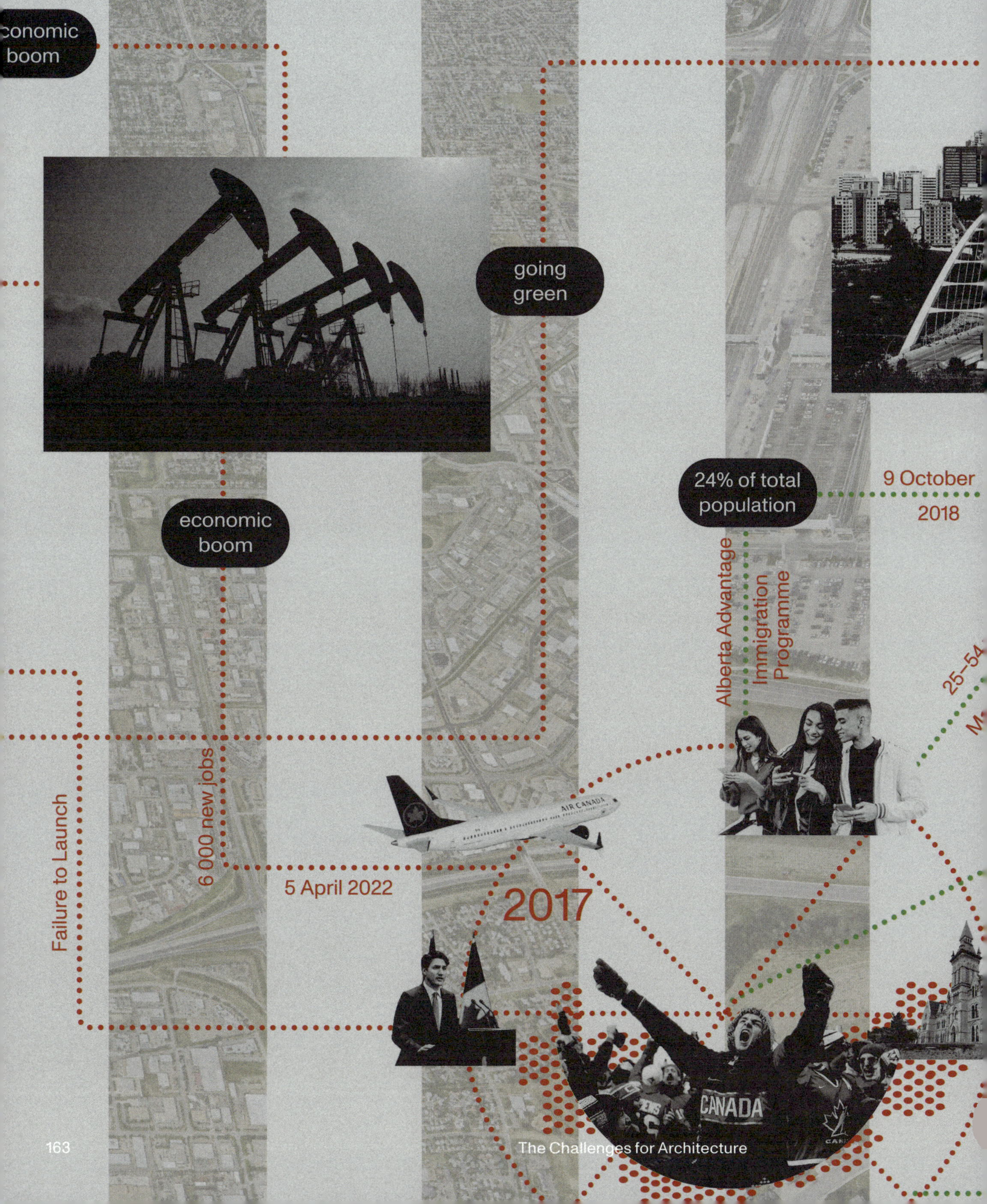
conomic boom
going green
24% of total population
9 October 2018
economic boom
Alberta Advantage
Immigration Programme
25–54
Failure to Launch
6 000 new jobs
5 April 2022
2017
AIR CANADA
CANADA

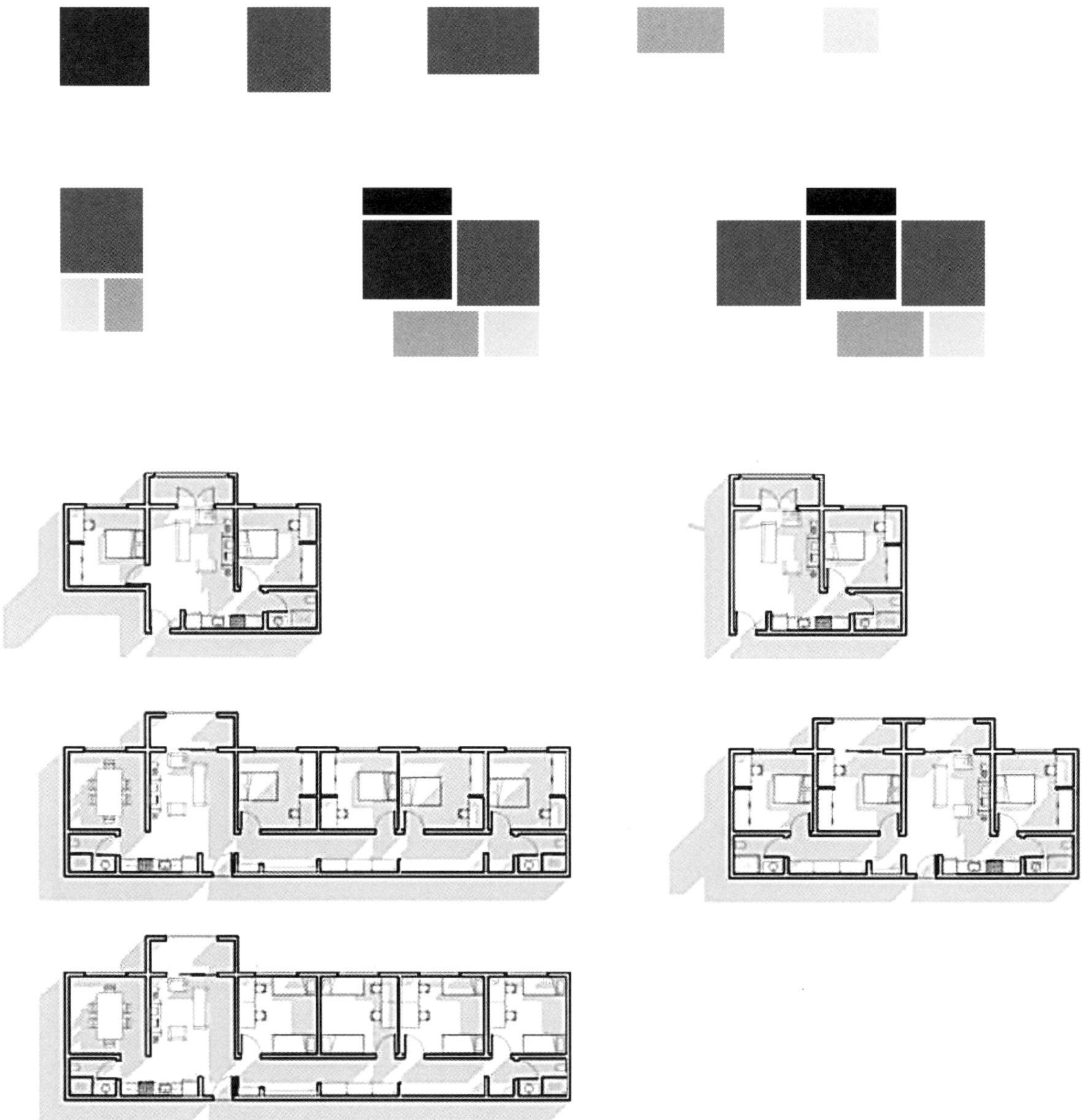

Unit typologies and configuration schemes

Wall-section concept, lower-level retail and upper residential stories

Typical block plan, uniform distribution

A Case for the Better

Bishrelt Solongo
and Brent Wafula

Site Area

21.93 Acres

Estimated Land Value

$42,774,000

Hard Construction Costs

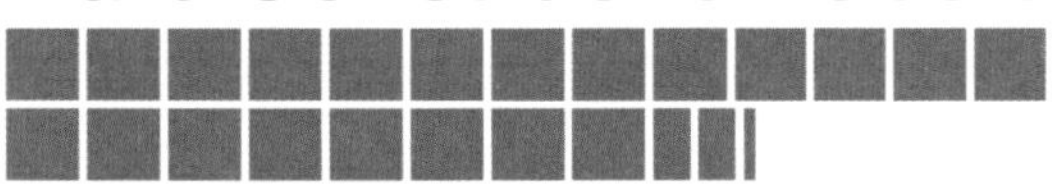

$212,337,984

Soft Construction Costs

$40,344,216

Residential Unit Count

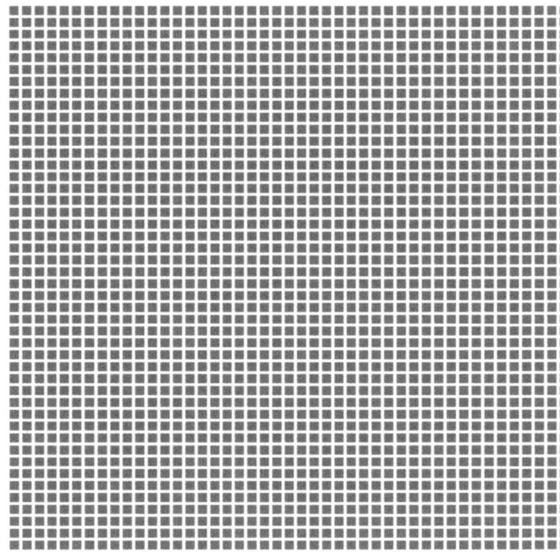

2070

Rent Range

$1,000–
$1,400

Residential Annual Gross Potential Revenue

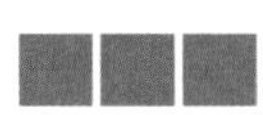

$30,164,040

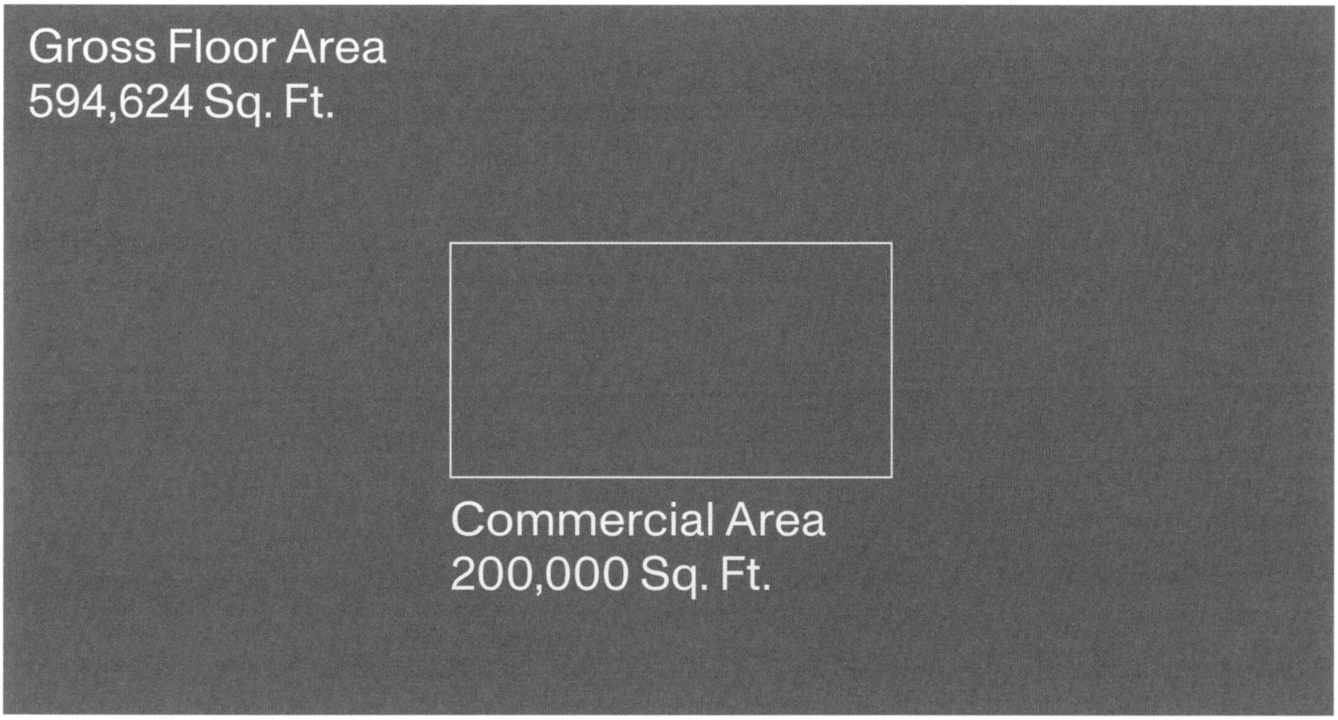

Non-residential Programming

Retail, Community Center,
Library, Rec. Facility

Commercial Annual Gross Potential Revenue

$60,000,000

Total Net Operating Income

$16,590,222

Reflections

Claire Weisz

Why the project "Oil, Land, People" became a way to understand the near future to a small circle of graduate students, faculty, and studio jurors is a matter of speculation. When we originally posed the studio prompt —that places are sometimes harbingers of larger forces —the relationship between a remote Canadian city and architectural education at Yale may not have been obvious. We hoped that access to the inner workings of a city that wasn't currently suffering from housing insecurity would unlock some new ideas and new models for architecture and urban development. With an economy fueled by oil and other forms of extraction, Edmonton might tell us a great deal about who we are as architects in the Anthropocene.

In development the constraints of financing and the limits imposed by political approvals and planning regulations are always location specific. The perspective of housing developer Marc de La Bruyère was invaluable in clarifying how an "affordable without public subsidy" development model works. Andrei Harwell, who has led studios and workshops in northern Scandinavian cities, most recently in Gothenburg, was intrigued to see how a different perspective on northern climate issues might lead to a better understanding of our own continent's northern building culture. Comparing other northern cities to Edmonton around some shared challenges like cold weather, extreme economic cycles, and diverse cultures was enhanced by the perspective of Farida Abu-Bakare, director of Global Practice at WXY, who sought to connect the studio with how immigration and indigeneity are important cultural forces to understand and consider in Canada. David Fortin, an Edmontonian professor of architecture at Waterloo and an architect of Indigenous Metis heritage, met with us during our visit to historic and contemporary social-housing models in Toronto.

Understanding how these future social and environmental pressures might influence ways of living allowed students to question current development models. This new awareness was enhanced by the juxtaposition between learning from designers working to advance Indigenous communities and housing-justice advocates who address the history of how the habitation of one culture is forced on another. These were the lessons learned during our visit to Toronto—that even projects deemed successful, such as Regent Park, were done at the cost of families and individuals who were never able to return. The work created by the studio, informed by these experiences, can be seen as both a translation of Edmonton's urbanity and as a demonstration in drawing, videography, and models of a variety of roles architects could play in urban development.

In 2022 Edmonton had not yet seen a housing crisis. By working on both the metrics and the models for affordability, the students recognized early on that the city was experiencing a housing gap primarily for those in need of support. Most residents at low to moderate income levels could afford rental or ownership options because the mean income is among the highest in Canada and home prices among the lowest. Two years later, and for the foreseeable future, almost every city in North America is experiencing a housing crisis. In a sense we taught a studio framed by the housing crisis in a city that has never experienced one and whose current political situation verges on systemic climate denial. There is also pressure to acknowledge that our cities are built on ancestral lands, and we must embrace the challenges and opportunities afforded to us by the long overdue reconciliation.

The combination of a cold climate, isolation, available land, open immigration policies, and the oil and gas industry's constant need for a skilled workforce has supported Edmonton's development. The students' projects reflect the shared understanding that no city should exist solely off the largess and the volatility of the fossil-fuel economy. Each student project looked for different ways for people to settle permanently in the city. The projects suggest that smaller spaces more connected to nature might be worth giving up for suburban homes and that being with those who are

Garneau Project and the Edmonton skyline, Maclab Development Group, Edmonton, Canada, Diamond Schmitt Architects, 2022

less mobile or independent, such as LGBTQ+ seniors, might provide reasons to develop a less car-centric neighborhood.

What continues to intrigue me about the Yale School of Architecture's Edward P. Bass Studio program is the chance for students to be exposed to today's real estate paradigms, specifically housing-development finance mechanisms. In the case of the Edmonton studio, the financial challenges of a fossil fuel–led economy and the developer's role in building housing to satisfy demand might have resulted only in projects that were greener and more regenerative versions of current standards. But that wouldn't have been enough considering the goals of the studio to better understand the culture of a place and the role of development. So what I now understand better through these design explorations are the values of this group of graduate architects.

To allow for this relationship to unfold serendipitously, the structure of the studio outlined several initial design exercises to individualize the students' experiences. The trip to Canada reinforced a community dialogue as part of a self-critical and self-motivated design process. The framework was meant to encourage each student to seek out the underlying problems before creating solutions for the typology, form, or program.

A travel studio, although focused on learning from a new place, is ultimately about gaining self-knowledge through one's own work in that new situation. For this reason, some of the strongest perspectives came from each student's project around culture, its origins, and its particularities. The students' initial autobiographical presentations, relating to a Canadian or Swedish artist or cultural event, were provocative. Each student found a connection to the concept of a cold climate and isolated city through film, music, art, or personal experience. Each student's creative work illuminated the less visible but influential culture of Edmonton: of immigration and livelihood, of winter isolation and making community. For example Bingyu He's lived experience creating a mise-en-scène for video games fueled his interest in creating appropriate ways to house a transitory digital workforce. Andrea Moctezuma Sanchez's interest in an immigrant filmmaker's use of winter led to an idea of development as an opportunity to live next to nature.

The studio directive to seek new strategies for building a sustainable future was purposefully set in the context of an economy where afford-ability is not primarily subsidized by the public. We proposed that the opportunity to evolve what can and should be subsidized through new development, when changes are asked of the public, might allow opportunities to address the gaps in social equity, environmental impact, and cultural opportunity. The work in this book demonstrates that these possibilities consider the role of design when harnessing public programs and market forces. To that end we all learned, and have a great deal more to learn, about the ways architects and developers understand what they could be doing in the future to create value for people to work together and find meaning in unexpected places.

Image Credits

Maclab Development Group
14, 15, 18, 19, 20, 29, 30, 31, 42, 174

WXY Architecture and Urban Design
36, 37, 38, 39, 42

Sentinel-2A satellite accessed via
Antti Lipponen on Wikimedia Commons
56

Värdefulla industrimiljöer i Stockholm
61

Arild Vågen accessed via
Wikimedia Commons
62

Edwin Whitefield accessed via
Wikimedia Commons
77 top

Toronto City Library
77 center, 93

City of Toronto Archives
94